DATE DUE

FEB 1 8 2003	
Freeport	
MAR 2 3 2005	
APR 1 6 2007	
AUG 2 0 2009	
FEB 0 5 2010	
6/13/15	

GAYLORD

PRINTED IN U.S.A

Culture and Customs of Haiti

Culture and Customs of Haiti

∽∾

J. Michael Dash

Culture and Customs of Latin America
and the Caribbean
Peter Standish, Series Editor

GREENWOOD PRESS
Westport, Connecticut • London

Library of Congress Cataloging-in-Publication Data

Dash, J. Michael, 1948–
    Culture and customs of Haiti / J. Michael Dash.
      p.   cm.—(Culture and customs of Latin America and the Caribbean, ISSN 1521–8856)
    Includes bibliographical references and index.
    ISBN 0–313–30498–X (alk. paper)
    1. Ethnology—Haiti.   2. Haiti—Social life and customs.   I. Title.   II. Series.
GN564.H2.D37   2001
306'.097294—dc21   00–033126

British Library Cataloguing in Publication Data is available.

Library of Congress Catalog Card Number: 00–033126
ISBN: 0–313–30498–X
ISSN: 1521–8856

First published in 2001

Greenwood Press, 88 Post Road West, Westport, CT 06881
An imprint of Greenwood Publishing Group, Inc.
www.greenwood.com

Printed in the United States of America

The paper used in this book complies with the
Permanent Paper Standard issued by the National
Information Standards Organization (Z39.48–1984).

10 9 8 7 6 5 4 3 2 1

For Nanou, my bright and morning star

Contents

A photo essay follows p. 79.

Series Foreword

"CULTURE" is a problematic word. In everyday language we tend to use it in at least two senses. On the one hand we speak of cultured people and places full of culture, uses that imply a knowledge or presence of certain forms of behavior or of artistic expression that are socially prestigious. In this sense large cities and prosperous people tend to be seen as the most cultured. On the other hand, there is an interpretation of "culture" that is broader and more anthropological; culture in this broader sense refers to whatever traditions, beliefs, customs, and creative activities characterize a given community—in short, it refers to what makes that community different from others. In this second sense, everyone has culture; indeed, it is impossible to be without culture.

The problems associated with the idea of culture have been exacerbated in recent years by two trends: less respectful use of language and a greater blurring of cultural differences. Nowadays, "culture" often means little more than behavior, attitude, or atmosphere. We hear about the culture of the boardroom, of the football team, of the marketplace; there are books with titles like *The Culture of War* by Richard Gabriel (Greenwood, 1990) or *The Culture of Narcissism* by Christopher Lasch (1979). In fact, as Christopher Clausen points out in an article published in the *American Scholar* (Summer 1996), we have gotten ourselves into trouble by using the term so sloppily.

People who study culture generally assume that culture (in the anthropological sense) is learned, not genetically determined. Another general assumption made in these days of multiculturalism has been that cultural differences should be respected rather than put under pressure to change. But these assumptions, too, have sometimes proved to be problematic. For instance, multiculturalism is a fine ideal, but in practice it is not always easy to reconcile with the beliefs of the very people who advocate it: for example, is female circumcision an issue of human rights or just a different cultural practice?

The blurring of cultural differences is a process that began with the steamship, increased with radio, and is now racing ahead with the Internet. We are becoming globally homogenized. Since the English-speaking world (and the United States in particular) is the dominant force behind this process of homogenization, it behooves us to make efforts to understand the sensibilities of members of other cultures.

This series of books, a contribution toward that greater understanding, deals with the neighbors of the United States, with people who have just as much right to call themselves Americans. What are the historical, institutional, religious, and artistic features that make up the modern culture of such peoples as the Haitians, the Chileans, the Jamaicans, and the Guatemalans? How are their habits and assumptions different from our own? What can we learn from them? As we familiarize ourselves with the ways of other countries, we come to see our own from a new perspective.

Each volume in the series focuses on a single country. With slight variations to accommodate national differences, each begins by outlining the historical, political, ethnic, geographical, and linguistic context, as well as the religious and social customs, and then proceeds to a discussion of a variety of artistic activities, including the press, the media, the cinema, music, literature, and the visual and performing arts. The authors are all intimately acquainted with the countries concerned: some were born or brought up in them, and each has a professional commitment to enhancing the understanding of the culture in question.

We are inclined to suppose that our ways of thinking and behaving are normal. And so they are . . . for us. We all need to realize that ours is only one culture among many, and that it is hard to establish by any rational criteria that ours as a whole is any better (or worse) than any other. As individual members of our immediate community, we know that we must learn to respect our differences from one another. Respect for differences between cultures is no less vital. This is particularly true of the United States, a nation of immigrants, but one that sometimes seems to be bent on destroying variety at home, and, worse still, on having others follow suit. By learning about other people's cultures, we come to understand and respect them; we earn their respect for us; and, not least, we see ourselves in a new light.

Peter Standish
East Carolina University

Preface

HAITIANS sometimes view with suspicion, or at least apprehension, books that attempt to interpret what is going on in their society. Their disquiet is justified by the countless works and articles that have been printed that purport to reveal the truth of what is going on in Haiti but end up being little more than titillating and melodramatic sensationalism. From the very outset, Haiti has been seen as a deviant and backward society. Attempts at objective or rational explanation of Haiti's society and culture were relatively few. Haitians themselves often contributed to this view of their country as odd or exceptional by insisting that no outsider could ever understand the peculiarities of their society. Much of that attitude has changed in recent times as Haiti enters upon a new period of openness to the outside world. Many Haitians now live on the outside and increasingly foreigners have a full and objective understanding of various aspects of Haitian culture. The U.S.-led multinational force that restored constitutional rule in Haiti in 1994 was made up of troops from neighboring Caribbean islands, suggesting an unprecedented rapprochment between Haiti and the Caribbean region.

Haitian society today is also less hierarchical and rigid than it was in the past. The turbulence that has marked Haiti's current transition to democratic rule is perhaps a symbol of convulsive transformations taking place in that society on all levels. The secular, politicizing effect of the Ti Legliz on the majority of Haitians, the more frequent use of the Creole language, and a more accommodating attitude to the vaudou religion on the part of the Catholic Church are all signs of an evolution from an inflexibly rigid social structure. There are signs of the presence of the outside world everywhere in

Haiti. These are as apparent in the now frequently seen transistor radios and
cassette players that are ubiquitous in rural Haiti, as they are in the adver-
tisements from magazines that paper the walls of cardboard shacks in Cité
Soleil. The horizons of the average Haitian have been transformed in recent
years. This is sometimes tragically apparent in the phenomenon of "boat
people" who attempt to get to Florida on overcrowded sailboats. Haitians
have always been poor but only in the last two decades have so many been
prepared to risk their lives to get to North America. Their awareness of the
outside world is acute.

It has been this area of literature and politics in Haiti's plight is a staggering one. Statistics can hardly convey the dimension of human suffering that exists in Haiti. Some of the most dramatic
examples of this human wretchedness are visible in the capital, Port-au-
Prince, where thousands live on the street and bathe in the gutters and where
thousands of children still die from measles and diarrhea. To concentrate
excessively on this reality is to miss a key element in Haitian culture. There
is something that is still ruggedly defiant about this rural, agrarian, and un-
industrialized culture. This ruggedness, which is often associated with its
landscape, is apparent in the arts of the imagination, which in Haiti are as
dynamic and prolific as they are inexplicable. This creativity is not only tied
to what some see as Haiti's uncontaminated primitive culture. The absence
of industrialization has indeed made Haitians very resourceful in adapting
traditional craft techniques to manufacturing a range of items for daily use.
However, Haitians have shown themselves to be equally resourceful in adapting the electronic media to suit their needs. Their creativity gets an added
boost today from Haitians in the Diaspora who with films, newspapers, and
popular music are changing the folkloric image of Haitian artistic expression
that has prevailed for too long.

It has not been easy to cover areas of contemporary Haitian culture. Not
enough has been written about Haitian cultural expression after the 1940s
and the burst of nationalist creativity that emerged at that time. It was also
difficult for me personally to leave the area of literature and politics in Haiti
in order to tackle relatively unfamiliar areas like Haitian art, the emergent
cinema, and music. In this regard I must thank Peter Standish for encouraging me to pursue the project despite my own feeling that I did not have
sufficient, all-round expertise to do the job. Because there is still little up-to-
date information available on the arts in particular but also on areas like the
media, cinema, and music, I must thank those who have in various ways
assisted in providing information. Pat Dunn of the West Indies Collection
of the University of the West Indies Library was helpful in providing Haitian
material from her collection. I must thank Serge Garoute and Maximilien

Larouche, who always knew the answers to questions, and Jean Claude Charles, who was my source of information in New York. Herman Van Asbroeck provided valuable information on Haitian art and photographs. Finally, I would like to thank Stella Vincenot for her assistance and for being a constant source of inspiration.

Chronology

1937   Massacre of thousands of Haitian cane cutters on the Dominican border

1941   President Lescot elected and beginning of the anti-superstitious campaign

1946   President Lescot is overthrown and Dumarsais Estime is elected

1949   The Exposition of the 200th anniversary of the founding of Port-au-Prince showcases Haitian culture

1950   General Magloire elected president, inaugurating a period of close relations with the United States

1957   Francois Duvalier comes to power after Magloire's overthrow

1964   Duvalier assumes presidency for life

1966   Indigenization of Haitian Catholic clergy

1971   Jean Claude Duvalier succeeds his father and declares new liberal policies; U.S. investments resume in Haiti

1980   Crackdown on press freedom and opposition groups

1986   Duvalier leaves for exile in France and a military junta assumes control of Haiti

1987   A new constitution is ratified, peasants are massacred at Jean Rabel and in November voters are gunned down during elections

1988   Military controlled election brings Leslie Manigat to power; he is overthrown later that year

1989   General Avril assumes the presidency

1990   President Aristide elected with 67 percent of the vote in UN-supervised elections

1991   Aristide takes office but is overthrown in September after seven months in office

1994   A U.S.-led international force lands in Haiti to restore constitutional rule and President Aristide returns to Haiti; coup leaders leave for exile in Panama

1995   Aristide steps down; new president, Rene Preval, and parliament elected

1999   President Preval dissolves parliament after almost two years of protracted squabbling between factions of the Lavalas movement

2000   Last U.S. troops leave Haiti and parliamentary elections are held after repeated delays in May; the party of former president Aristide, who is expected to win presidential elections in December, sweeps the parliamentary and local government seats in the face of opposition protests over irregularities

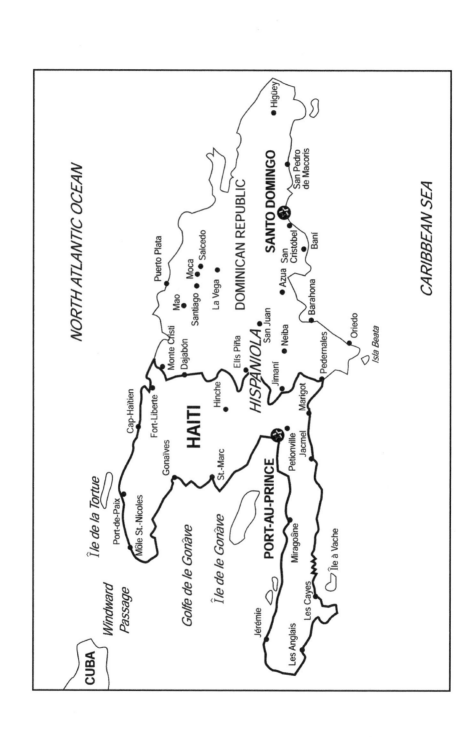

1

Context

IF THERE is one feature of Haitian geography that has marked Haiti's history and the impression that it has inevitably left on visitors to that country, it is the ruggedness of its mountainous landscape. Almost every book written on Haiti makes reference to these mountains, majestic or forbidding depending on the writer's point of view, that dominate the landscape. For instance, in one of the best-known novels written about Haiti, *The Comedians* by Graham Greene, the main character on returning to Haiti is struck by the daunting spectacle of

> the huge mass of Kenscoff leaning over the town that was as usual half in deep shadow; there was a glassy sparkle of late sun off the new buildings near the port which had been built for an international exhibition in a so-called modern style. A stone Columbus watched us coming in.[1]

The petrified figure of the discoverer, the town's fraudulent modernity, and the menacing shadow of the mountain typify many visitors' reactions to Haiti.

Christopher Columbus, after sighting the island of Hispaniola on December 5, 1492, is reputed to have demonstrated the forbidding nature of the island's terrain to King Ferdinand and Queen Isabella by crumpling a sheet of paper in his hand and tossing it on the royal table. Mountains cover approximately two thirds of the land area of Haiti. The Spanish ultimately found the land uninviting, and in the seventeenth century it became the haunt of buccaneers, infamous because of the pirate stronghold of Tortuga off the northern coast. The French, to whom the western third of the island was ceded in 1697, could establish control over only the towns and the few coastal plains, thereby contributing to the slave revolt that began in 1791 and ended French control of St. Domingue in 1804. Napoleon also failed in his attempts to reimpose French rule largely because of the mountainous terrain. Subsequently, the first black republic in the Western Hemisphere, and the only country created by a successful slave revolt in recorded history, was named Haiti from the Taino word meaning "land of mountains" and has managed to maintain a defiant isolation from the rest of the world.

Haiti gives the impression of vastness and impenetrability because of its extremely mountainous terrain, but it occupies only one third of the island of Hispaniola, the other two thirds of which is occupied by the Dominican Republic, and its area measures 10,714 square miles. It is bounded on the north by the Atlantic Ocean, on the south by the Caribbean Sea, and it shares an eastern border with the Dominican Republic. Haiti's closest neighbors are the islands of Jamaica and Cuba. The shape of the Haitian land mass is also quite remarkable: it is marked by two peninsulas, one in the north and the other in the south, that run east to west, further aggravating communication within Haiti. These two peninsulas have been described as jaws, with the Gulf of Gonâve as its wide-open mouth, within which the island of La Gonâve appears on the verge of being swallowed up. Mountains cover about two thirds of Haiti's land area, reaching their highest elevation in the Pic de la Selle (8,793 feet) in the southeast. There are four plains that form the country's main areas of agricultural activity.

The most important northern town, Cap-Haïtien, is situated on the Plaine du Nord, and Haiti's capital, Port-au-Prince, is on the cul-de-sac. Most of Haiti's main towns are ports, and some are still only easily accessible by sea because the mountain ranges make internal communication so difficult. The country is crisscrossed by numerous streams and rivers, but they are unpredictable in that they can just as easily stop running during dry seasons as well as overflow during torrential downpours. The largest and most important river is the Artibonite, which flows through the Artibonite plain and empties into the Gulf of Gonâve.

If Haiti's topography is dramatic, it is also desolate. It has been described as an ecological nightmare. When Haiti was sighted by Columbus, it was more than 90 percent forested. Today only 2 percent of Haiti is forested, as trees have been cut down for firewood since 70 percent of Haiti's energy needs are met by charcoal (which is created from wood). The supply of arable land decreases by 3 percent annually. Deforestation and soil erosion are the major hindrances to rural development in Haiti. A comparison is always made with the western two thirds of the island because Haiti's rural population is 35 percent greater than that of the Dominican Republic but has less than 40 percent as much arable land.

Haiti is the only country that is considered Latin American but whose language and culture are predominantly French and whose population is predominantly of African descent. Haiti's ethnic and linguistic makeup contrast with that of its neighbor. It is not only in this area that the Dominican Republic is distinct from Haiti. The literacy rate, life expectancy, and other social indicators compare unfavorably with the figures from the Dominican Republic. This is not surprising, since Haiti has the lowest per capita income in Latin America and is the poorest country in the Western Hemisphere. This represents a dramatic change for Haiti, which was once the richest French colony.

COLONIAL HISTORY

The legendary wealth of the French colony of St. Domingue depended on Europe's insatiable appetite for sugar, which had been introduced to the island earlier by the Spaniards. It was also the Spaniards who first turned to Africa for slaves to work on the sugarcane plantations after the decimation of the indigenous population through forced labor and disease. The inhabitants of the island Columbus called Hispaniola were called Tainos or Arawaks. They were described as peaceable and gentle, but it was these very qualities that made them vulnerable to exploitation, as the Spaniards soon put them to work in their gold mines. By the middle of the sixteenth century the indigenous population, which was originally estimated at one million, had been reduced to a few hundred on the entire island.

With the supply of gold speedily running out, and distracted by the quest for gold in the colonies of Peru and Mexico, Spain ceded the western third of the island, which would be known as St. Domingue, to the French. Colonization of St. Domingue was at first very unpromising. The colony was first populated by former buccaneers who made very unlikely farmers. It was only with new migration from France and the growing realization that sugar, coffee, and cocoa would flourish in the colony that the era of prosperity began. The next big obstacle was that of labor, as there was no native labor left to be exploited. The French, like their Spanish predecessors, then turned to African slavery, and St. Domingue became the destination for slave ships leaving the African coast. No one is sure how many African slaves made it to Haiti, but toward the end of the eighteenth century the slave population numbered half a million. The white population numbered 36,000 at the same period. This population was as famous for its ostentatious and lavish lifestyle as for its cruelty to the slaves. The expression "as rich as a Creole" was commonly used in France. However, severe punishment, harsh discipline, and torture were inflicted so that control could be maintained. The legendary cruelty of the plantation owners also guaranteed such intense resentment that in less than a century after claiming St. Domingue, the French faced an insurrection that would eventually cause them to relinquish control of their wealthiest possession.

There were signs as early as the 1750s of the explosive possibilities latent in St. Domingue. Slaves called maroons, who escaped into the inaccessible mountainous terrain, would attack vulnerable plantations from time to time, but in 1758 they found a leader in Makandal, who used the vaudou religion to build a network of followers and succeeded in poisoning the water supply for the plantations of the Plaine du Nord. The spark that really ignited the explosion in the colony was the French Revolution, and the social class that was responsible was the *gens de couleur*, or free coloreds. This group numbered 28,000 and included all freed persons of African blood. They were the children of white planters and female slaves, and when liberty was granted they were entitled to French citizenship under the Code Noir (Black Code) emanating from Louis XIV. This class, often well educated and even owning slaves themselves, flourished particularly around the southern town of Jérémie and saw St. Domingue as their home.

Despite the liberal provisions of the Code Noir, there was strong resentment of the free coloreds by whites in the colony. As noted by Moreau de Saint-Méry, a visitor to St. Domingue on the eve of violent insurrection, this resentment against people of mixed blood was caused by

> their growing demand for equality with the whites—to be addressed with the respectful "Monsieur" before their last names, to have full participation in the professions and the officer class in the army and to enter the government service.
>
> The whites resisted such steps more determinedly than before, partly because there were now so many of these new rivals. The circumstance that so many mulattoes, who were nearly all freedmen, were coming to own plantations, especially in the Western and Southern parts of the country, made the whites uneasy.[2]

With the outbreak of the French Revolution, the mulattoes hoped that the increasing discrimination against them would end and that their rights as established by the Code Noir would be reinstated. However, when a young mulatto named Ogé, educated in France, returned to St. Domingue and led a demonstration in 1791 with his friend Chavannes in Cap Français to demand the restoration of rights for the free coloreds, they were both seized and brutally executed. The white planters had thereby irrevocably alienated a class that could have sided with them but whose hostility was now made absolutely certain.

Precisely at this time, the slaves of St. Domingue revolted against their masters. This insurrection has become legendary because it was planned at a vaudou ceremony held in a forest called the Bois Caiman during a violent storm and was led by a priest named Boukman. The indiscriminate slaughter that followed was unprecedented in its savagery, and the planters did not have a chance against the pent-up fury of half a million slaves. The uprising of the slaves was viewed as a welcome event by the freed coloreds, who began to see that equality with the whites would come only through force. In the confusion that followed, two figures emerged as leaders of the insurrection: the colored general Rigaud, who led the mulattoes, and the ex-slave Toussaint Louverture, who led the half-million blacks. By 1796 Toussaint emerged as the only leader with the power to control St. Domingue and inspired enormous devotion among his followers. The only group that distrusted him was the mulattoes, because of their inability to accept an ex-slave who now wielded such power. However, a brief conflict between Toussaint and Riguad saw Toussaint emerge as the supreme leader of the ex-colony and, at least for the time being, mulatto power was broken in Haiti.

The years that followed would mean the consolidation of power by Toussaint and the spread of his reputation for astuteness, leadership, and military skill. He was governor general of St. Domingue from 1799 with the reluctant consent of the French and by 1801 had conquered the Spanish colony on the east of the island. Under his absolute authority, the violence and anarchy of earlier years ended and prosperity was restored. The restoration of peace and stability meant that former slaves were ordered back to work on the plantations. The use of a repressive labor system to force the newly liberated masses back to the plantations was one of the early ironies of the pre-independence period. Nevertheless, economic success was one of the major achievements of Toussaint from 1799 to 1802. As one well-known account of Toussaint's role in the Haitian revolution described it:

Personal industry, social morality, public education, religious toleration, free trade, civic pride, racial equality, this ex-slave strove according to his lights to lay their foundations in the new State. In all his proclamations, laws and decrees he insisted on moral principles, the necessity for work, respect for law and order, pride in San Domingo, veneration for France. . . . Success crowned his labors. Cultivation prospered and the new San Domingo began to shape itself with astonishing quickness.[3]

However, despite his phenomenal success, the rise of Napoleon in France would inevitably lead to the demise of Toussaint in Haiti.

The period between 1802 and 1804 was a crucial time for revolutionary St. Domingue, as the retaking of the once prosperous French colony was a key part of Napoleon's plan to establish a New World empire. Napoleon sent his brother-in-law, General Leclerc, with a formidable military force to St. Domingue and attempted to persuade Toussaint that Leclerc should be allowed to succeed him as governor with the guarantee that slavery would not be restored in St. Domingue. However, after his arrival with his fleet in January 1802, Leclerc's advances were repelled and war broke out between Toussaint's army and Leclerc's forces. Toussaint made the fatal error of not arming the ex-slaves and trusted his generals, who eventually surrendered to Leclerc's advancing forces. Resistance to the French was eventually broken at the battle of Crete à Pierrot, and soon after Toussaint, lured into a meeting with Leclerc, was seized and sent to a dungeon at the Fort de Joux in the Jura Mountains in France, where he died in 1803.

Ultimately, Leclerc's mandate was to restore slavery in St. Domingue. This plan would never be carried out, as yellow fever took a tremendous toll on his forces. The news that he planned to reestablish slavery also helped to re-create resistance to the French. Toussaint's black generals joined forces with the mulattoes and fought Leclerc's now weakened forces. By the end of 1802 Leclerc himself was dead, and the conflict entered a particularly barbaric phase as Rochambeau, who had succeeded Leclerc, massacred every black or mulatto he could lay his hands on, and Toussaint's generals responded with similar brutality. By the end of 1803 Napoleon had abandoned his now catastrophic New World adventure, and Rochambeau gave up this futile struggle, retreating to the Mole St. Nicholas, the same point at which Columbus had landed 300 years earlier, inaugurating European domination of Hispaniola.

INDEPENDENCE

On January 1, 1804, St. Domingue, devastated by years of unrelenting strife, was declared independent and renamed Haiti by the black general Jean Jacques Dessalines in the town of Gonaïves. Motivated by absolute hostility to France, the new constitution forbade any white person from owning land in Haiti and stipulated that all Haitians, regardless of color, were to be called black. Dessalines, in a fateful act, created the Haitian flag by seizing the French tricolor and tearing out the white band in the middle. Henceforth, Haiti's flag would be red and blue. Symbolically, with the whites gone, a struggle would ensue between blacks and mulattoes as to who would rule the world's first independent black republic and the second independent state in the Western Hemisphere.

Outside of Haiti, it is the genius of Toussaint Louverture that is admired. And even before his wretched demise, the English poet William Wordsworth had composed a sonnet to honor his legacy. Within Haiti, however, it is the fierceness and violence of his subordinate, Dessalines, that inspire approval. This admiration, which is evident in place names, postage stamps, and the national anthem, stems from the fact that he symbolizes the final break with the colonial power. The Dessalinian state also epitomized the more absolutist features of Toussaint's rule, which would mark public life in Haiti for the forthcoming decades and lead to the notorious cultural and political plurality that has divided independent Haiti. The revolutionary process that created the Haitian state was based on the need to put an end to plantation slavery and to promote the ideal of liberty for all. However, it seems clear from the first attempt at a Haitian state in Louverture's short-lived tenure as governor general that the state would replace the old plantocracy and remain attached to controlling the plantation system and that the liberated slaves saw themselves as an emergent peasantry. On the one hand, the freed slaves would be part of the machine of the state, and on the other hand, independence was defined in terms of personal freedom. Independence would put power exclusively into the hands of the new military state and would create important contradictions with the rest of the nation.

Apart from the contradiction between state and society, political independence had produced an internally divided state whose differences had been glossed over by the shared animosity toward the French. The fundamental division was between *anciens libres* (those free before independence) and *nouveaux libres* (those free after independence) and goes back to the pre-independence days when the *gens de couleur* saw their fate as different from that of the slaves on the plantations. Bitter rivalry between these groups in the period after independence would lead the Haitian state from crisis to crisis. For instance, very early in the rule of Dessalines, tensions emerged because of mulatto distrust of a Dessalines, a *nouveau libre* who had proclaimed himself emperor for life. Consequently, Dessalines began to be seen by the mulatto elite as an upstart, as uncivilized and brutish as the outside world made him out to be because of the massacre of whites in the period preceding independence. Within three years of its creation, the Dessalinian state was in crisis. Dissatisfaction spread not only among the lighter-skinned generals, who resented his authority, but also among the masses who disliked his militaristic domestic and agricultural policies, since Dessalines had basically divided the nation into workers and soldiers. By 1806, insurrection spread through the mulatto strongholds in the south and west of Haiti, and he was assassinated at an ambush on Pont Rouge. On October 17 of the same year, after being in power for two years, Haiti's liberator and self-styled emperor lay dead.

The new Haitian state was caught in a tangle of contradictions. On one hand, a militarized agricultural state and a revival of the plantation system were the only immediate ways to ensure economic prosperity. On the other hand, the black labor force saw itself as a peasantry and justifiably avoided what they saw as the neo-colonial state. In all this, the refusal of the western world to recognize Haitian independence and the attendant desire to reimpose economic dependence on Haiti would exacerbate internal tensions. The emergent Haitian state with its legacies of massive illiteracy, internal dissent and economic precariousness suffered greatly from this ostracism. For instance, the refusal of recognition by the Vatican would "cripple the Haitians' chances of building a solid and wide-ranging system of formal education" since in Catholic nations "religious orders had always been the backbone of the formal education system."[4]

But no missionaries and teachers would be forthcoming from Rome until a concordat was signed with the Vatican in 1860. Similarly, the United States, which formally recognized the independence of other countries in the Western Hemisphere that had liberated themselves from Spanish domination by 1822, withheld recognition of Haiti until 1862. The precariousness of diplomatic relations with Haiti within the hemisphere was inevitably tied to U.S. disapproval, as was the attitude of European governments, who began to accept U.S. dominance over the hemisphere and whose attitudes to Haiti were arguably tied to U.S. ostracism. It also comes as no surprise that the expelled colonial power, France, would not grant formal recognition until 1825, after the payment of a massive indemnity of 150 million francs as compensation to dispossessed French planters. Neocolonial dependence meant that Haiti would not be easily accommodated in any global system, and with few international allies its sovereignty would be violated at will during the nineteenth century by warships of foreign powers seeking redress for their citizens' interests.

The fourteen years following Dessalines' murder were marked by dramatic internal fragmentation in Haiti. Henri Christophe became Haiti's next ruler because of military seniority and soon acquired a reputation for grandiose projects such as the construction of a palace, Sans Souci, modeled on Versailles and the impregnable fortress of the Citadelle Laferriere. Before long, his authority was contested by mulatto generals whose strongholds were in the west and south of the country. The mulattoes created a republic in the south under General Pétion while Christophe was crowned king in the north and ruled over a semi-feudal state. Unlike Christophe in the north, Pétion, because he was light-skinned and an *ancien libre*, made concessions to the masses in the form of land grants. After Christophe's overthrow and Pétion's death in 1818, General Boyer united the country under mulatto control in 1820 and continued Pétion's practice of granting land to the peasantry and members of the army. By Boyer's presidency it had become clear that Haiti could not construct a viable agrarian economy from the ruined plantation system. As a rural peasantry became established, the infrastructure left by the French decayed, and remote rural districts became increasingly isolated. Whatever the color or ideological inclination of these four generals who ruled Haiti, their legacy was a militarized state that would dominate public life for years to come. As one scholar put it:

> The army was the great power in the country, for the new state was a military one. Since fear of a return of the French required the maintenance of a large standing army, Dessalines made a virtue of this apparent necessity, using the soldiers to enforce discipline among the cultivators. On whom else could he rely for his local administration? Here again, the decision of a leader fixed the direction of Haitian life for decades to come. It is agreed by commentators that overmilitarization was the bane of nineteenth century Haiti.[5]

The second and equally important legacy of this early period of independence is collapse of the plantations and the full-blown emergence of a peasantry in Haiti by the overthrow of Boyer in 1843. In this regard, Haiti in the nineteenth century was profoundly different from the rest of Latin America, whose post-independence experience was characterized by a land-owning aristocracy and peons who worked their large estates. Haiti's aristocrats did not own most of the land, and the peasants were not peons because they owned or squatted on their own small farms. This single fact would contribute to creating what James Leyburn defined with a little exaggeration as a caste system in Haiti, since the two strata are more closely related than one would expect in a traditional caste system. As the rural areas began to be dominated by this unplanned and alienated peasantry, an elite established itself in the towns and jealously guarded its distinction from the rural peasantry.

> Under the complaisant rule of Boyer, the people of color came to regard themselves as the unquestioned elite. Their claim was shared, though not always acknowledged by a small number of blacks (mostly from the north) who had been anciens libres in colonial St. Domingue or noblemen under Christophe.[6]

Much of the history and politics that follow is shaped by the contradictions of this social order: an illiterate, distrustful peasant majority; a numerically tiny elite divided by rivalry based on color; and the absence of anything like a middle class to exert a moderating or stabilizing influence on this precarious situation.

Increasingly, as the century wore on, the survival of a militarized elite would depend on the exploitation of the peasantry. With the large estates falling into disuse and the peasantry refusing to participate in regimented, state-run agriculture, the elite turned to the state as a means of consolidating their status by extracting whatever surplus they could from the peasantry. This is crucial to the period between 1843 and the U.S. occupation of 1915, as the military elite turned its attention away from the plantation system and became increasingly involved in the ruthless pursuit of political power. In these seventy-two years, political confusion increased as twenty-two heads of state came to power, all of them military men, of which fourteen were deposed by insurrections and three were killed in office, the last of whom was hacked to death in the capital by an angry mob. The most infamous presidency during this period must be that of Faustin Soulouque, who was chosen because he was a nonentity in the military. With his accession to power however, Haiti began a twelve-year nightmare. The brutishness of this regime both led to further economic ruin for Haiti and encouragement to Haiti's critics abroad, who saw the new state as simply lapsing into savagery without white control.

The seeds of national disaster were planted in this period as politics increasingly became a game of rivalry among urban elites and was marked by insurrection, economic failures, and parasitism. Indeed, the general tendency, as was rather disastrously exemplified in the case of Soulouque, was to put in power a black general who would be a puppet for the interests of a light-skinned elite or oligarchy. This phenomenon, called a *politique de doublure*, or government by understudies, dominated the nineteenth century as black generals came to power manipulated by powerful mulatto interests behind the scenes. The general turned on his mulatto patrons, crowned himself emperor, and created a paramilitary force called the *zinglins*, an early model for the Tonton Macoutes. Under Soulouque, Haiti's image abroad sank to an all-time low as it became increasingly portrayed as a tragicomic example of black decadence. Meanwhile, the lives of the majority of the population were in no real way affected by the vagaries of Haitian politics. The two features that mark the political culture of Haiti between the fall of Boyer and the arrival of the Americans are (1) a massive growth in the state apparatus as (2) more and more sought to enrich themselves from the state. These parasitic state appendages included an army forever increasing in size, state employees, and various other professionals. As they grew in size and in their parasitic demands, the economy was stagnating and the peasantry becoming increasingly impoverished. Haiti therefore entered the twentieth century with the majority of its population as cut off from the outside world as it was from its own leaders and, at the other end of the spectrum, with a bloated, nonproductive state apparatus that had no interest in investment in the land or changing in any way whatsoever the lot of the peasantry.

The period from 1843 to the U.S. occupation of 1915 was one of steady descent into chronic disorder. Changes in head of state, constitutional crises, revolution and counterrevolution were the surface manifestations of a socioeconomic system in crisis. Never in this period would productivity approach the standard of the early post-independence period. By the turn of the century, Haiti had become a land of small-scale peasant tillage with an external trade that was appropriated for the exclusive use of a tiny elite. A marginalized and silenced peasantry, then, was ruled by a state divided by competing interests, and rival factions constructed on an economic base of ever-shrinking returns led, by the beginning of the twentieth century, to political chaos and vulnerability to foreign interests. Between 1900 and 1915, after a hundred or so years of independence, Haiti faced a succession of incompetent short-term presidents. Between 1911 and 1915, a rapid succession of revolts managed to place six presidents in office. None naturally served out his full term, and the last of the six was killed by a mob in Haiti's capital. In the face of economic ruin, the Haitian oligarchy turned to heavy borrowing abroad, as much from France and Germany as from the United States. Indeed, desperation ran so high that there was even talk in the commercial sector of the desirability of annexation by the United States, whose domination of the northern Caribbean was by then almost total. It has been observed that:

Within Haiti there was, in fact, division of opinion. Foreign merchants were not the only ones prepared to believe that a thorough cleansing and a new start might be for the public good. No Haitian could openly advocate American intervention, but there seems to have been an undercurrent of opinion in that direction, though of necessarily uncertain proportions. As men of property or merely as government employees, the elite had nothing to gain from chronic disorder and instability.[7]

U.S. OCCUPATION

The debate concerning the desirability of intervention, in any case, was overtaken by U.S. expansion in the Caribbean and Central America at the time. This strategy was justified by the use of the Monroe Doctrine, which argued for an exclusive U.S. sphere of influence in the Americas. U.S. policy at the time was based on strategic interests, particularly in relation to the recently completed Panama Canal and the need to keep Europe, by then embroiled in World War I, out of the hemisphere. The case for U.S. control in the region was described as follows:

> It is usual to speak of the Caribbean Sea and the Gulf of Mexico as the American Seas, and to consider them as part of our life and practically within the control of this nation. It is necessary that we should glance at the great seas and appreciate how they and the Canal are hemmed in by islands, which would become a menace to our commerce in case of war or hostility on the part of the nations of Europe.[8]

The actual pretext for the occupation of Haiti came on July 28, 1915, when a mob seized then-president Vilbrun Guillaume Sam from the French Legation and lynched him. Fearing the worst, various diplomatic missions asked the United States whose gunboats were conveniently anchored at Haiti's capital, to take control, and that night Admiral Caperton ordered his marines onto Haitian territory, initially to protect the lives of foreigners and its own citizens. They would stay nineteen years, representing a second phase of colonial rule for Haiti.

Despite the fact that the occupation was often justified in terms of bringing peace, progress, and democracy to a country that had reverted to savagery, the immediate effect of the intervention was to increase the power of the state and the overall dependency of the country on outside interests. After restoring order through military means, the first act of the occupying power was to install a puppet president and to legitimize the U.S. presence by having the Haitian legislature approve a convention making Haiti a protectorate of the United States. A new constitution was also passed, giving the president increased powers and allowing foreigners to own land in Haiti. Militarism in Haitian society, already a massive obstacle to development, was further enhanced by U.S. use of martial law, military courts to judge opponents to the occupation, and the imposition of forced labor in the countryside, which led to short-lived Caco revolts under the leadership of a former army officer, Charlemagne Peralte. Peralte and his 2,000 or so peasant insurgents were unable to perform the feats of the army of liberation that led to Haitian independence in 1804. In 1919 he was shot to death in his own camp, and the pacification of the Haitian countryside was complete. With the end of organized armed opposition, a new army, called the *Garde d'Haiti*, would be formed that would bear no relation to the army that liberated the nation in 1804 and would exert a disastrous influence on the post-occupation period.

The occupation sought to reform an economy that for a century had become inefficient and to stabilize a society that continued to lack cohesiveness. The United States created vocational schools along the lines of the Tuskegee Institute, Booker T. Washington's school for vocational training for blacks in the United States, and increased expenditure on agriculture. They introduced various amenities like a telephone system in the towns and the road linking Cap-Haïtien with Port-au-Prince. Significant measures in health and sanitation were introduced. Bridges and roads were built, and the Haitian currency stabilized. However, many reforms were introduced so insensitively that they would be rejected once the United States was no longer in control. Quite often, the results of U.S. policies were very different from what was originally stated. Under the occupation, the United States controlled the collection of import duties, for instance, and it could also set budget priorities. Therefore, most of the money collected was spent on debt repayment to the United States, which would have been drawn mostly from peasant farmers. The United States thereby simply exacerbated a phenomenon that had plagued the Haitian economy since 1843, the extraction of surplus from the peasantry by a nonproductive state.

Perhaps the greatest single lasting effect of the occupation was the centralizing of state power in Port-au-Prince. The Caco uprising would be the last such phenomenon that any Haitian president would have to fear until the fall of Jean Claude Duvalier in 1986. Rural ports gradually lost their importance because of the new road system, and the countryside became more dependent than ever on Port-au-Prince. The centralization of the collection of custom duties in the capital may have helped to reduce corruption, but it increased the importance of Port-au-Prince. This centralization also reinforced the power of merchants in the capital. Whatever the negative effects of regionalism in the past, and they are not difficult to pinpoint, it did provide a countervailing force to absolute state control. Since administrative and economic centralization was accompanied by military centralization, no president in the post-occupation period could resist using the concentration of state power that he had under his control.

The Haitian state needed no lessons in the use of military force to enforce its authority. Yet this is precisely what the United States managed to accomplish by 1934. All the authoritarian practices it originally criticized, it ultimately legitimized. Through the professionalization of the Haitian army, the disarming of the peasantry, and the creation of a military apparatus and a system of intelligence gathering controlled from the capital, the United States created a force with which it would maintain formal and informal links after the end of the occupation. Even though their stated intent was otherwise, the U.S. Marines demonstrated by their example the involvement of the army in the day-to-day running of the country. Even more unfortunately, the example was being set by an army that occupied the country. To this extent the Haitian army that emerged from the occupation often behaved like an army of occupation rather than a national army. The problems later posed by the Haitian military were already present in embryonic form in the Garde d'Haiti, which was created during the occupation. One scholar noted that

[one] cannot overemphasize the fundamental political difference between the Garde and the army that was dismantled by the marines. . . . Haiti's first army saw itself as the offspring of the struggle against slavery and colonialism. . . . Because of its stated role, because of its origins, and because of Haiti's position in the world, the nineteenth century Haitian army believed it had been assigned a national mission, even though history may have proved it wrong. . . . In sharp contrast, the Haitians Garde was specifically created to fight against other Haitians. It received its baptism in combat against its countrymen. And the Garde, like any army it was to sire, has indeed never fought anyone *but* Haitians.[9]

In 1930 Stenio Vincent was elected president in the first elections in which the Marines did not interfere. Vincent led Haiti to what he called its second independence when the Marines finally left in 1934. By then officials in Washington had begun to grow tired of the occupation, and the geopolitical rationale of its continuation no longer existed. Haiti's second independence had arguably much in common with its first. The occupation left Haiti with

very much the same destructive socioeconomic problems that it inherited
from its colonial past. Beneath the veneer of political stability lay the same
old problems of a militarized society: the ostracism of the peasantry and an
elite divided by class and color rivalry. However, very much in the same way
that rival factions of the elite joined ranks in 1804 to expel the French, the
United States in the nineteen years of the occupation managed to do what
no Haitian president had been able to do: unite the elite across the color
divide. Indeed, the 1920s and 1930s in Haiti saw a nationalist cultural and
literary resurgence that was unprecedented. This was an intellectual renaissance based on national and racial consciousness, and it spawned widespread
debate as to whether Haiti's identity was French or African, whether its
politics should be socialist or fascist, and, most important, it gave peasant
culture an unprecedented intellectual and literary emphasis. However, much
of this momentum would be lost as soon as the unifying force of the white
foreign invader was no longer present and old color and class contradictions
resurfaced. Material improvements also soon decayed as roads fell into dis-
repair and, for the mass of the rural population, life in the remote interior
continued as before.

The occupation left Haiti in the hands of the mulatto elite, and the two
light-skinned presidents between 1934 and the revolution of 1946 did much
to antagonize not only the black elite and newly created professional class
but also the intellectual avant-garde because of their authoritarian tendencies
and the concentration of power in the hands of the mulatto elite. Mulatto
insensitivity under these presidents reached an all-time low with the massacre
of black Haitians in the Dominican Republic by the Trujillo regime in 1937.
This massacre evoked relatively little response from the Haitian government.
Equally bad was the persecution of the vaudou religion by Vincent's successor, Elie Lescot, in 1941 and the number of concessions made to U.S. com-
panies for various business ventures in Haiti. When Lescot attempted to
prolong his presidency by altering the constitution, strikes broke out in Port-
au-Prince, and in 1946 a student-led protest forced Lescot into exile and the
military stepped into the vacuum in the form of Major Paul Magloire, who
organized elections that brought to power a black president, Dumarsais Estimé.

The Estimé presidency is important both in terms of the emergence of the
army as a power broker in Haitian politics and the political manifestation of
Haitian negritude in the choice of a black president. It was argued that a
black president was the most authentic expression of the need to regain black
dignity after U.S. and mulatto humiliation. The Black Nationalist ideology
of *noirisme*, or Haitian negritude, became a pervasive intellectual movement

that would eventually sweep Francois Duvalier to power. The roots of *noir-isme* can be traced not only to anti-Americanism during the occupation but also to a reaction among black Haitians and radical intellectuals against the contempt shown by mulatto rulers in the post-occupation period. Estimé's mandate was based on resentment of the mulatto faction, but he never went far enough, as far as the noiristes were concerned, in fulfilling this mandate. The noiristes were further frustrated when he was ousted in 1950 and re-placed by General Magloire, who was seen to be just another example of the old nineteenth-century *politique de doublure*. When Magloire was forced into exile because of attempts to prolong his term, it was felt that someone was needed to complete the Estimé revolution. It was in such a context that the candidacy of Francois Duvalier won the approval of the noiriste camp, par-ticularly and crucially the support of noiriste army officers. The army-supervised elections meant that Duvalier had the support of the Haitian military in 1957. More important, however, he had the support of the old Estimé faction and its deep conviction that a black president with close ties to the masses and the emergent black middle class was what was needed to complete the revolution of 1946, which had as its ultimate goal the destruc-tion of mulatto rule in Haiti.

The story of Francois Duvalier's presidency is that of the transformation of a mild-mannered country doctor into a semi-divine absolutist leader. The word "Duvalierist" has become synonymous with "dictatorial," attesting to the nature of the dictatorship that Duvalier's presidency created between 1957 and 1971. As we have seen, there was nothing unusual about Haitian presidents assuming dictatorial powers. However, the extreme nature of the Duvalierist state makes it the most disturbing manifestation of state power in Haitian history. Duvalier consolidated state power by first of all neutral-izing all the institutions in civil society that could pose a threat to his regime. Schools, churches, trade unions, universities, and the media were all under-mined as priests were expelled, journalists tortured, and intellectuals forced into exile. Paranoid about security and having witnessed Estimé's downfall because of the army, Duvalier did not ignore the Haitian army in this process of neutralization. As he got rid of generals considered untrustworthy and closed the military academy, he enlisted the help of the United States in training soldiers loyal to himself. By far his most dramatic strategy was the creation of a civilian militia, officially called the Volontaires de la Securité Nationale (Volunteers for National Security) but popularly known as the Tonton Macoutes, as a countervailing force to keep the army in check. (The Tonton Macoutes refers to a Creole expression for a traditional bogeyman who kidnaps children in his "macoute," or knapsack.) This civilian militia was not only a parallel institution but was drawn from a wide cross-section of Haitian society, providing a network of intelligence gathering and nation-wide intimidation of any potential opposition. It was this manipulation of state violence that protected the Duvalier regime from both internal desta-bilization as well as external invasion. It would be erroneous to believe that what distinguished Duvalierism from previous dictatorships was simply the ruthless and efficient manipulation of state terror. Violence alone could not provide security for this regime. Rather, it was the size of the social base that it could draw on as well as the shrewd manipulation of popular culture that made Duvalierism unique and eventually turned it into a hereditary dicta-torship.

Duvalierism, as much as anything else, was aimed at ending mulatto dom-ination of the state. The noiriste ideology spawned in the 1930s and the support of the *authentiques* of Estimé's regime guaranteed the allegiance of the emergent black middle class as well as support among the urban poor and the peasantry. Duvalier's experience as a country doctor also played a role in this strategic sensitivity to influential members of the rural commu-nities. Crucial to the endurance of the Duvalierist state were these links it fostered with rural Haiti. Duvalierism certainly encouraged the links between the Tonton Macoutes and vaudou, and it used the peasant religion to en-hance Duvalier's own aura of mysticism and infallibility. His very inscruta-bility, the somber formality of his dress as well as his secretiveness, all encouraged associations with the vaudou god, Baron Samedi, the keeper of the cemetery. The links with vaudou priests also helped him to keep abreast of happenings outside the capital. Forever the master of the dramatic sym-bolic gesture, Duvalier changed the color of the Haitian flag from red and blue to red and black to represent Haiti's African heritage. The same intent lay behind the creation of the statue of the unknown maroon (fugitive black slave) as a symbol of Haiti's black, revolutionary past. During Duvalier's presidency, Emperor Haile Selassie of Ethiopia visited Haiti, and a main street was named for Martin Luther King, Jr., after his assassination. Duvalier used these occasions to propagate the ideology of international black con-sciousness even though it was a facade for state plunder that caused his regime to be labeled a "kleptocracy."

Even though Duvalier deliberately used his ideology of a racial and na-tional mystique to create a hermit state that thrived on isolation, no Haitian regime can be expected to survive without the complicity of outside elements or at least tacit approval from the United States. Duvalier's relations with the Vatican are a vivid example of his ability to shrewdly manipulate outside elements and also carry out his own ideological reforms. Since 1959 Duvalier had shown overt hostility to the foreign clergy by expelling priests and closing religious institutions.

It has been noted that Duvalier and a number of the men he brought to his government in 1957 had been critical of the role played by the Roman Catholic church in Haiti and in particular of the control which it exercised over leading educational institutions in the country.[10]

This criticism was partly based on the belief in vaudou as the repository of Haiti's authentic values. Conflict with the Church reached a high point with the expulsion of Bishop Robert in 1962, which earned the president expulsion from the Catholic Church. In retaliation, Duvalier had the entire Jesuit order expelled for subversive activities in 1964. However, Duvalier was able to negotiate a settlement with the Vatican in 1966 that brought an end to this protracted feud and saw the return of the papal nuncio but also allowed Duvalier to have a hand in the appointment of a local clergy on whose support he could count.

Outmaneuvering the United States would be a more complex operation for Duvalier since Washington's blessing was crucial to his regime's survival. From early in his presidency there was mutual suspicion between the Haitian and U.S. governments. The United States was becoming alarmed at civil rights abuses, and Duvalier believed that Washington had a hand in attempts to topple his regime by invasion. However, after the success of the Castro revolution in overthrowing the U.S.-backed regime of Batista in Cuba, Duvalier became adept at playing on American fears of subversion in the Caribbean. The United States had some difficulty supporting a government that by 1961 had abandoned all pretense of democracy and by 1964 had declared Duvalier president for life under a new constitution. However, in the atmosphere of the Cold War and alarmed by civil war in the Dominican Republic, the United States softened its hostility to Duvalier. By the end of the 1960s aid was once more forthcoming, and diplomatic pragmatism prevailed. Duvalier used his crudely anti-leftist stance to both appease Washington and liquidate any local opposition. For instance, 1969 marked a bloody offensive against the Haitian Communist Party, and it happened to coincide with a much-publicized visit of the then New York governor, Nelson Rockefeller. In no time investment in Haiti was restored. Haiti began to produce every baseball used in the national baseball league. By Duvalier's death in 1971, Washington was willing to provide naval vessels, which patrolled Haitian waters to ensure a smooth transition of power from Papa Doc to his son, Jean Claude Duvalier.

In the early 1970s the Duvalier dynasty was not given much chance of success because of the singularly unprepossessing nature of the obese and inexperienced Jean Claude Duvalier, or "Baby Doc," as he was called by the skeptical media. He claimed at the outset that he would lead an economic revolution in Haiti, but he generally continued the initiatives of his father even though there was a relaxation in the use of state terror and a toning down of the noiriste rhetoric. The "economic revolution" really meant attracting foreign capital, thereby giving a boost to the local bourgeoisie, who would benefit from these new investments. Much of the fear and hostility felt by this class for the older Duvalier was dissipated under Baby Doc, as they could now share in the profits from this new injection of capital, particularly in the light assembly industry. To seal the new coalition between the new regime and the commercial class, Jean Claude Duvalier in an elaborate ceremony married Michele Bennett, the light-skinned daughter of a speculator who had grown wealthy under the regime. The marriage symbolized the new phase of Duvalierism with its strategic alliance with the commercial elite. The choice of Michele Bennett, with her non-Duvalierist connections, was seen by hardline Duvalierists, or the "dinosaurs" as they were called, as a betrayal of Papa Doc's noiriste politics. Michele Duvalier—who was soon to be proclaimed "The First Lady of the Republic," thereby usurping the president's mother—helped to foster the image of economic liberalism and reconciliation with old enemies.

Despite an increase in American investments, essentially in assembly plants using cheap, nonunionized labor, and the atmosphere of economic liberalism, little real development came to Haiti. The light assembly industry could not on its own transform Haiti, since most of the population in the countryside in no way benefited from increased employment in this area, and the disparities in income and amenities between the capital and the rural area only grew larger. This would turn out to be a disastrous error for Jean Claude Duvalier, who was slowly but surely weakening the very social structure that had kept his father's regime in place. Furthermore, insensitivity to the plight of the peasantry reached an all-time low with the order to eradicate all local pigs because of an outbreak of swine fever. By 1984 more than a million animals belonging to low-income peasants were slaughtered and replaced by U.S. government–supplied imported animals that the peasants could not afford to raise. This further exacerbated the appalling plight of rural Haiti, whose misery had become evident from the increasing numbers of "boat people" trying to leave Haiti beginning in the mid-1970s. This did not in itself bother Duvalier's government, but it was becoming an international embarrassment for the regime, which in 1981 signed an agreement with Washington to allow for the forcible repatriation of illegal Haitian immigrants by the U.S. Coast Guard. Desperation also drove the poverty-stricken peasantry to migrate to the Bahamas and the Dominican Republic, in the latter instance to work under the supervision of the Dominican military in near-slavery conditions on the sugar plantations.

In the meantime, further problems were in store for the regime from outside as the neglect of human rights and economic mismanagement and corruption were attracting the criticism of the Carter Administration and later the Reagan Administration in Washington. President Carter had expressed strong disapproval of Baby Doc's human rights record. Being anticommunist was no longer good enough, and future aid would be tied to respect for human rights. The liberalism that resulted from these reforms was short-lived as the advent of a Republican administration, led by Ronald Reagan, suggested less sensitivity to such issues as human rights. The liberal facade disappeared after Reagan's inauguration, but Washington's disquiet now came from a different source. Foreign aid was increasingly diverted away from infrastructural improvements and into the pockets of the Duvalier regime. In order to deal with this new criticism of his regime, Jean Claude Duvalier appointed Marc Bazin, a World Bank official, as finance minister. He did not last six months, thus signaling the regime's determination not to respond seriously to pressures to modernize.

Baby Doc's regime was, therefore, facing a number of contradictions, both internal and external. The alienation of the mass base of the movement would prove to be as dangerous as the vacillating attempts to appease various administrations in Washington. One of the most dramatic instances of the regime's attempts to present an acceptable image to the outside world, which backfired, must be the visit of Pope John Paul II in 1983. On arrival in Haiti, the pope spoke explicitly about the need for social reform, taking as his theme the slogan "things must change." His words did not fall on deaf ears, as for some time progressive parish priests in Haiti who were inspired by liberation theology had been organizing groups of their parishioners for discussion of issues like social change and human rights. This movement, known as the Ti Legliz or "little church," was instrumental in organizing grassroots movements that would play a leading role in the riots that broke out in 1984. The Duvalier government had badly misjudged what it thought would be a public relations operation, and the pope's visit added further impetus to this movement toward change. As the grassroots churches became more militant, Christian radio stations, especially Radio Soleil, also became more explicit in their demands for reform.

By the mid-1980s the economic situation had grown progressively worse. Persistent droughts, a rapacious state, and the crisis of a country that exported little and depended massively on foreign assistance contributed to further deterioration of Haiti's weak economy. Tourism went into irreversible de-

cline when the U.S. Center for Disease Control in Georgia declared that
Haitians were a high-risk group for the AIDS virus. The assembly industry
was not making much of a contribution to the national economy and was
simply taking advantage of the government's invitation to exploit the Haitian
people. Resentment in rural areas was already high because of the eradication
of the entire pig population in Haiti. By now cracks were beginning to appear
in the Duvalierist dictatorship that were never previously apparent. The Haitian people began to react by resorting to violence in the food riots of 1984
and 1985 in Cap-Haïtien and Gonaïves. The formidable Duvalier dynasty
was now pitted against an irreversible tide of people power. The crumbling
of Duvalierism would also give increased independence to the institutions of
the church and the army, which would be locked in conflict over the direction
Haiti would take after 1986.

Twenty-eight years of Duvalierism had exacerbated the cleavage between
nation and state that had been inherited from independence and that now
made Haiti the poorest, most socially polarized country in the Americas. The
statistics provided by various aid agencies are "starkly eloquent":

> In 1985 public expenditure on education amounted to one per cent of
> Gross Domestic Product, or 43.70 per capita; public expenditure on
> health in the same year was estimated at 0.9 per cent of GDP, or 43.44
> per capita. For each secondary school teacher in Haiti there were 189
> members of the security forces, while for every secondary school there
> were 35 prisons. The country's infant mortality rate stood at 124 per
> thousand . . . average life expectancy in 1982 was calculated to be 48
> years. And beyond the statistics there stood the simple truth that the
> great majority of Haitians were hungry and many were starving.[11]

Driven as much by desperation as politicization by the Ti Legliz, demonstrations became more frequent and violent. They were met in 1985 by a
predictable show of force from the regime. Radio stations were shut down
and the army began to fire on demonstrators. Repression reached its height
with the shooting of four schoolchildren in November 1985. As demonstrations grew, Washington began to distance itself from the regime, further
encouraging the demonstrators. The army—with little reason to remain loyal
to a regime that had humiliated it for years, and dependent for its security
on the ubiquitous Tonton Macoutes—began to grow restless, and there were
rumors of a possible coup d'état by late 1985. By February 1986 Duvalier
had lost control of the countryside and was putting up a brave show in the
capital, Port-au-Prince, which as the seat of the state remained immune from

the crisis affecting the nation. However, support had begun to dwindle from both Duvalier's traditional supporters and his foreign advisors. It was becoming clear that Duvalierism as an extreme manifestation of the authoritarian state in Haiti could not survive much longer.

For the first time since 1804 the Haitian people, silenced and ostracized for so many decades, made it abundantly clear that they wanted a radical change in politics. The reasons for their courageous stand in the 1980s are complex. They have as much to do with desperation as they do with influence by the progressive elements in the Church, the expansion of communications and the media in particular, and the tentative efforts at liberalization under Duvalier. The people were literally given a voice through the small radio stations, usually manned by Catholic priests, which broadcast in Creole. Revolutionary sermons were circulated on cassette tapes. Indeed, one of the more remarkable features of the mass movement that eventually brought an end to Duvalierism was the absence of a central leadership. Mobilization was effected through neighborhood committees, peasant organizations, and self-help groups. This was an advantage because no person or persons could be identified and arrested to remove the source of authority and discourage supporters. However, it also meant that there was no coherent strategy for what was a genuinely popular movement. It also created a vacuum in leadership of the anti-Duvalierist movement after Jean Claude's departure.

The White House, which had begun to put distance between itself and the increasingly precarious Duvalier regime, showed its eagerness to see Duvalier depart by prematurely announcing that he had fled the country. However, the fact that Duvalier did not leave until a week later is significant, since it is during this period that he and his advisors set about organizing a Duvalierist government that would succeed him. Jean Claude and Michele Duvalier finally left in the early hours of February 7, 1986, on a U.S. Air Force cargo plane to join in exile in France a diaspora that had been created by his father.

AFTER DUVALIER

The news of the departure of the Duvaliers brought jubilation to Haiti. In an almost Dessalinian gesture of defiance, the statue of Columbus was toppled and tossed into the sea. The mood then changed to revenge as homes of prominent Duvalierists were attacked and looted. Suspected Tonton Macoutes were necklaced with burning tires. A crowd made its way to Papa Doc's tomb, demolishing the mausoleum, but there was no coffin inside. This did not mean that the last vestiges of Duvalierism had disappeared after the euphoria of the first days had subsided. Haitians found that they were faced with a military junta led by General Henri Namphy, who had been handpicked by Duvalier and who would be less than willing to respond to their demands for *dechoukaj*, or rooting up the Duvalierist past.

The official position, corroborated by the U.S. State Department, was that the interim governing council would prepare Haiti for democratic elections. As aid from Washington for the junta increased, the confrontation between Duvalier loyalists and grassroots activists also intensified. A massacre of peasant activists in Jean Rabel in July 1987 attested to the brazen self-assertion of Duvalierists a little over a year after Baby Doc's departure. In a referendum in 1987 a new constitution forbidding Duvalierists to participate in elections for ten years and removing the supervision of elections from army control was approved by an overwhelming majority. In the elections of November of that year, however, Duvalierists thugs, with the support of the army, massacred voters, and the elections were called off. The Haitian army was asserting its old role as power broker and in January 1998 held its own elections, which were marked by a low voter turnout and the "victory" of the army-approved candidate, Leslie Manigat.

The intervention of the United States, France, and the Vatican in negotiating the departure of Jean Claude Duvalier both slowed down the revolutionary process in Haiti and elevated the army once more to a position of prominence in Haitian politics. The next few years would witness bloody confrontations between state militarism and a reanimated civil society, witnessed by a largely indecisive international community. The one thing that was needed to consummate the victory of the popular movement was a free and fair election. The army would again and again frustrate this desire so much so that the slogan "We cut down the tree but have not got rid of the roots" became popular among those advocating democratic change. The situation was further complicated by the fact that many who offered themselves for election did not represent the aspirations of the majority, and the grassroots movement did not have national leadership.

After twenty-nine years of political inactivity, Haiti now witnessed the frenzied explosion of new political parties, human rights organizations, and labor unions. The political parties were invariably led by men who had spent the last two decades in exile and had some difficulty reintegrating themselves into Haitian society. Even those who had remained, sometimes at great personal risk, seemed marginalized by the rapid and often violent evolution of events in Haiti. As traditional politicians got pushed to the sidelines or compromised themselves by their links with the military, the center stage was occupied by radicals of grassroots organizations, in particular the Ti Legliz.

The emergence of a credible leftist movement in Haiti was not welcome news for Washington. It became even more unpalatable when leadership fell to the ascetic and charismatic parish priest Jean Bertrand Aristide, who preached a message that was as inflexible as it was idealistic. The new Haiti must provide for all its people so that, as he put it, they could move "from misery to poverty with dignity." This could only be achieved outside the control of the traditional oligarchy and international capitalism. Aristide was immediately identified as a leftist firebrand and miraculously survived attempts by the Haitian army and the Catholic Church to silence him. When, under international pressure, the military was finally forced to accept democratic elections under UN supervision in 1990, the outspoken and increasingly influential Aristide won by a massive majority.

Aristide's victory in these elections meant that the will of the majority had finally prevailed, and for the first time since the departure of Baby Doc four years earlier there was jubilation in the streets. His Lavalas ("Flash Flood") movement had come to power bringing with it a loose coalition of peasant groupings, labor unions, and human rights organizations. Despite its popularity, the Aristide government was always precarious. Neither the elite nor the army nor conservative elements in Washington were pleased with the dramatic turn of events in Haiti. Aristide's presidency would last a mere seven months and was marked as much by populist gestures as by an often fiery rhetoric aimed at alienating the elite. In September 1991 the army, under General Raoul Cedras, staged a coup that ousted President Aristide and drove him into exile in Venezuela. With the Lavalas leadership in exile or in hiding in Haiti, a savage and systematic repression of the slums and countryside was conducted by the military. Thousands were killed in the next three years as the army tried to rule exclusively by force of arms. It was incapable of consolidating power and unable to persuade the international community, which had condemned the coup and imposed an embargo, that its actions were justified.

Ultimate resolution of the Haitian crisis was left in the hands of the United States, which remained reluctant to go beyond symbolic condemnation. However, a combination of the economic effects of the embargo and military repression drove thousands of Haitians to take to small boats in order to flee their country. They were forcefully repatriated by the U.S. Coast Guard, using the old agreement signed with the Duvalier government. It was this wave of boat people that finally forced action by the United States. The plight of poor Haitians driven to desperation on the high seas caught the world's attention and, more important, the attention of liberal elements as well as African American political leaders in the United States. Enormous pressure was put on the Clinton Administration in 1994 to have the de facto coup leaders removed. The way was cleared for the United States to use military force to remove the coup leader through a UN resolution in July authorizing the use of "all necessary means" to remove the army. Direct invasion was forestalled by an accord negotiated by former President Carter with the Haitian military, allowing for the unopposed entry of the American forces. In September 1994, seventy-nine years after Admiral Caperton landed his marines in Port-au-Prince, 20,000 American troops were deployed in Haiti.

The United States led an intervention, but the return of President Aristide in October 1994 did not bring any immediate solution to Haiti's problems. From the outset, moral issues were complicated as the coup leaders were allowed to go into exile, and initially the U.S. troops allowed the local police and army to persist in human rights violations. Rumors spread of Washington's involvement with the repression during President Aristide's exile as CIA links with one of the most notorious paramilitary organizations, FRAPH (Revolutionary Front for the Advancement and Progress of Haiti), and its death squads were revealed. Perhaps most significantly, the U.S. Army never attempted to disarm the population. In the meantime, Haiti had been further impoverished because of the embargo and the basic elements of civil society crushed because of military repression. Haiti's recovery was also slowed down because the Aristide who returned was not the one who was driven into exile. Aristide had now become a politician. He did achieve the abolition of the Haitian army in 1995 but accomplished little else. He remained personally very popular, and in the elections of June 1995 the Lavalas coalition swept home with a massive majority. However, when he attempted to extend his term of office by the period of his exile he was forced to step down, and Rene Preval, with a last-minute endorsement, came to power in an election marked by a low voter turnout.

Returning Haiti to constitutional rule by restoring Aristide to power and then establishing the Preval presidency by constitutional means turned out to be the easy part. The real difficulty now is how to restore an economy after the more than ten years of turmoil that followed the Duvaliers' departure. The treasury is empty and more than half the work force is idle. Security and justice are also persistent problems, given the moral ambiguities of amnesties for coup leaders and the refusal of the U.S.-led multinational force to disarm the population. Most important, ideological contradictions have arisen between the Aristide people-based Lavalas platform and the international aid agencies, which have put together millions of dollars in aid based on a restructuring and a liberalization of the Haitian economy. Frustration abroad at Aristide's stubborn insistence on a rigidly populist position has turned to alarm as he created his own party to facilitate reelection in the year 2000, thereby splitting the Lavalas coalition and paralyzing parliament as his supporters consistently block efforts at privatization of the Haitian economy and any attempt to implement the structural adjustment program. This has created an increasingly disillusioned population, which has seen the quality of their lives deteriorate further because of the political impasse and the consequent hesitation of financial institutions to release a multimillion-dollar aid package. The crisis has led the secretary general of the United Nations to report that "the consolidation of democracy in Haiti has been undermined."[12]

As the 200th anniversary of Haitian independence approaches, the fact that Haiti was the only island to achieve its independence by force of arms fades in the light of the face of a continuing political crisis that may have a tragic effect on the fledgling democracy established in the wake of the end of the Duvalier dynasty. After decades of turmoil and misrule, Haiti is undergoing a very difficult transition to constitutional rule and democratic government. Haitians still find themselves battling for economic survival and caught up in social unrest and political violence. Flawed elections and political infighting brought down the government of Rosny Smarth in June 1997. No prime minister has been appointed since then because ratification by Parliament has been withheld since opposing factions from within the Lavalas movement make agreement on a successor to Smarth impossible. Parliament as well as the Lavalas movement have been severely weakened by this political standoff, and an indecisive René Préval seems incapable of ending this political gridlock.

This parliamentary stalemate has cost millions of dollars in aid from international financial institutions. A revitalized economy is an essential aspect of the creation of a democratic Haiti. However, there is no sign that the feuding factions are prepared to heed the warnings of impending doom. The fate of democracy in Haiti is made even more precarious because an increasingly disgruntled population shows less and less interest in the electoral process. Voter turnout in elections, held since the restoration of constitutional government, has been alarmingly low. An old political culture based on divisiveness, an inability to compromise, and a lack of genuine concern for the mass of the Haitian people still haunts Haitian politics. Signs of the dire nature of the situation are the continuation of the UN mandate to provide security, as there is no confidence in the inexperienced police force that has replaced the army. In addition, more and more Haitians wish to leave their country; the boat people phenomenon shows signs of beginning again.

Equally disturbing is the fact that the only thing preventing the local economy from collapsing is the money that comes in from remittances from Haitians abroad.

Frustration with the Haitian crisis turned to alarm as President Preval in January 1999 effectively dissolved Parliament by insisting on upholding an electoral law that set January 11 as the end of the term for the majority of Haiti's legislative and municipal officials. Preval's action has been seen by his critics as a coup d'état and as paving the way for the return of his mentor Aristide. For some, Parliament, which has not endeared itself to the Haitian people, brought the action upon itself, and there is general distrust of all politicians, who seem to be motivated by little more than self-interest and greed for power. The period leading up to long-delayed national elections has been marked by political infighting, snags in voter registration, street protests, and a wave of violence that seems to be politically motivated. In the meantime more than $300 million in World Bank loans and International Bank funds remain undisbursed as there is no parliament to ratify these loans. Haiti may well turn out to be Washington's saddest foreign policy disappointment. As the century drew to a close, Haiti, already the poorest country in the Western Hemisphere, slipped to the 159th position on the UN human development index. In 1990, when President Aristide was elected, Haiti was ranked 124th of the 175 countries surveyed.

NOTES

1. Graham Greene, *The Comedians* (Harmondsworth, England: Penguin, 1967), 43.

2. Louis Elie Moreau de St. Mery, *A Civilization That Perished: The Last Years of White Colonial Rule in Haiti*, trans. Ivor Spenser (Lanham, MD: University Press of America, 1985), 257.

3. C.L.R. James, *The Black Jacobins* (New York: Vintage Books, 1963), 24.

4. Michel Rolph Trouillot, *Haiti, State Against Nation: The Origins and Legacy of Duvalierism* (New York: Monthly Review Press, 1990), 51.

5. James Leyburn, *The Haitian People* (New Haven CT: Yale University Press, 1966), 36–37.

6. Ibid.

7. Ludwell Lee Montague, *Haiti and the United States 1714–1938* (Durham, NC: Duke University Press, 1940), 193.

8. Ibid, 34.

9. Trouillot, *Haiti, State Against Nation*, 105.

10. David Nicholls, *From Dessalines to Duvalier* (Cambridge, England: Cambridge University Press, 1979), 221.

11. James Ferguson, *Papa Doc, Baby Doc* (Oxford, England: Blackwell, 1987), 90.

12. Don Bohning, "Haiti Risking Loss of Support As Crisis Festers" *Miami Herald*, October 8, 1998.

2

The People and Society

HAITIANS are justifiably proud of the fact that theirs was the only successful slave revolution in history and that success was achieved by defeating an expeditionary force from one of the most powerful armies that existed at the time, that of Napoleon. Pride in being the only country in the Caribbean and Latin America to found a nation from the struggle against slavery is manifest in statues of the founding fathers of Haitian independence in the Champ de Mars in Port-au-Prince. Three of the heroes of independence, Toussaint, Christophe, and Dessalines, were actually born into slavery.

This racial and national pride is further reinforced by the fact that Haiti's revolution was not seen in exclusively national terms. The Haitian revolution was seen as a model for other liberation movements, especially in Latin America. Such a principle lay behind the visits of revolutionaries like Francisco Miranda and Simón Bolivar to Haiti between 1815 and 1816.

Haiti's revolution was both national and hemispheric in its conception. It was not simply Haiti's emergence as a black state that created difficulties for European powers. It was the ambition of the founding fathers to have a global impact that was most worrisome to European powers, which had in the past been able to accommodate various maroon enclaves in places like Jamaica and Surinam. Consequently, international hostility to the fledgling republic was guaranteed from the start. It is not surprising, for example, that when the independent states of Latin America held their first-ever meeting in Panama in 1825, Haiti was not even invited. This conflict between Haiti's self-image and international reluctance in bestowing recognition has haunted relations between Haiti and the outside world since independence.

Haiti has always had the lure, or perhaps revulsion, of the extreme case. The belief that the unrestrained ex-slaves would soon lapse into savagery haunted most of the writing about Haiti in the nineteenth century. This idea acquired a new currency with the U.S. occupation as a pattern of sensationalist journalism emerged, fed by stories of sorcery and cannibalism in Haiti. Such writing did much to justify the occupation in the eyes of the U.S. public. The advent of Duvalierism in 1957 meant the reinforcement of the stereotypes of Haiti as a land of danger, mystery, and evil. For the next three decades these images of Haiti would persist. In the 1980s Haiti's image abroad further deteriorated with the dramatic increase of refugees, or boat people, arriving on the coast of Florida and the mistaken belief that Haitians were carriers of the AIDS virus. Haiti's reputation as the land of the strange and the supernatural was perpetuated by the ethnobotanist Wade Davis, whose book *The Serpent and the Rainbow* presented a picture of Haiti as the land of black magic and zombies. Not surprisingly, the book was made into a popular horror movie in 1988.

Curiously, along with many of these often racist depictions of Haiti, there emerged another tendency that was single-mindedly negrophile in its celebration of the marvelous strangeness of Haitian culture. The most widely read and influential of the books that painted Haiti as a primitive Eden was William Seabrook's 1929 travel book, *The Magic Island*. Seabrook depicted an elemental and earthy Haiti and inaugurated a vision of throbbing drums and gyrating bodies that became the stock in trade of adventure stories and travelogues. In the 1940s the image of Haiti as a society whose values were profoundly different from those of the Western world made that country attractive to European surrealists because of their interest in dreams, the unconscious, and the occult. This interest culminated in the visit of the leader of the French surrealist movement, André Breton, to Haiti in 1945. It was Breton's vigorous defense of indigenous cultural values that eventually helped to overthrow the Lescot regime in 1946, as the president was seen as representative of oppressive foreign interests. The ideas of the marvelous and the magical that were spread by Breton also were of enormous literary value and artistic interest to Haitians in their representations of their own culture.

Objective, scientific accounts of Haitian culture, especially Haitian popular culture, have always been difficult to come by. The first serious efforts by foreign anthropologists and ethnographers to document Haiti's popular culture were done in the 1940s in the works of Melville Herskovits, Harold Courlander, and Alfred Metraux. After the fall of the Duvalier dynasty in 1986, a number of informed and dispassionate accounts of Haiti began to emerge in the press. Haitians began to be treated as a people attempting to establish a democratic state after decades of misrule. Haitian characters were also sympathetically treated in works of fiction. Two of the most important of these were Russell Banks' *Continental Drift* and Brian Moore's *No Other Life*, published in 1986 and 1993, respectively.

Even though, in general, the perception of Haiti is that of a country of black magic and repulsive politics, the truth about Haitian society is necessarily more complex. The most striking feature of Haitian society is the wide separation between the rich and the poor or, more accurately, between elite and peasant masses in that country. The gap is so visible in terms of color and culture that an American sociologist described Haiti as a caste society. This peculiar social situation resulted from old divisions between *anciens libres* and *nouveaux libres*. Most of the former were mulatto and owned property, whereas the latter were the black former slaves. Distinction between these two groups was legally abolished with independence, and Haitian identity was constructed in terms of black dignity. However, suspicion and hostility has divided both groups. Economic and color differences between free coloreds and ex-slaves persisted after independence and gradually eroded national unity in the post-independence period. The crucial act of parceling state lands by Alexandre Pétion meant the end of large-scale agriculture in Haiti by his death in 1818. His successor, Jean-Pierre Boyer, saw the emergence of a peasantry cut off from the people of color who began to see themselves as an elite.

THE ELITE

To this extent Haiti resembles Latin American countries, which exhibited one general feature: an aristocratic class that lived very differently from the peasants or peons in their various countries. In Haiti, however, the class lines became even more marked because the elite did not own most of the land and the peasants did not work for them directly. This meant that the two groups developed along different lines socially and culturally. Social distinctions, which first became apparent during the Boyer presidency (1820–1843), became established in the seventy-two years that followed and were further reinforced when the marines invaded in 1915. Despite the fact that during the period between the downfall of Boyer and the onset of the occupation Haiti was ruled by black military heads of state, members of the mulatto elite established themselves in business and monopolized areas such as the law, the arts, and various government functions like the foreign service and secretaries of state. During this time the Catholic religion played a role in reinforcing class divisions, since the schools that the elite attended were Church-run and generally adopted a Francophile position regarding culture.

The U.S. occupation reversed almost a century of political tradition and put the elite back in power, but did little to change their mentality. Not only was political office invariably seen in terms of personal advancement or class interests, but many of the well-intentioned reforms instituted by the Americans, like improved infrastructure and vocational training, were seen by the elite as threats to their political and social dominance. It was not long after the departure of the Marines in 1934 that social antagonism reared its head again. Indeed, the most flagrant example of autocratic elite rule came with the election of President Lescot in 1941. Mulatto rule seemed so entrenched at this time that an American sociologist writing in 1941 concluded that "for the present and the near future it is safe to say that there will be no more black non-elite presidents."[1] This prediction turned out to be dramatically incorrect. Lescot was driven from office in 1946 amid charges of using his office to feather his own nest and denying justice to the black masses of Haiti. This effectively meant the end of mulatto control of Haitian politics. Lescot was succeeded by Estimé, who saw himself as the champion of the working class. He was replaced in 1950 by a black general, Paul Magloire, in an army-controlled election. In 1957 Francois Duvalier, a noiriste ideologue, was elected to the presidency, defeating the mulatto candidate, Louis Dejoie.

In his desire to eliminate any semblance of an opposition to his regime, Francois Duvalier turned against two centers of elite power in Haiti: the Catholic Church and the business community. The Church, with its foreign francophile clergy, was seen as the main ideological instrument of domination of the mulatto elite. This attack on Catholicism was closely linked to Duvalier's desire to reform Haiti's educational system. In order to promote racial pride, give greater prominence to national history, and bestow greater recognition on the Creole language, Duvalier demanded a modification of school curricula. This policy was bitterly opposed by the Catholic clergy and the mulatto elite, which saw concessions in these areas as major threats to their dominant position. Duvalier also targeted the powerful members of the business community, who in the past used the business strike and their family connections in the civil service to put pressure on governments. The business community was no match for the Macoutes, who were unleashed on them by Duvalier. He also used the support of the extensive Syrian and Lebanese community to break the stranglehold of the traditional elite's power. The destabilizing of the elite reached its bloodiest point in 1964 after the failed invasion by mostly mulatto guerrillas of the southern peninsula. Reprisals were swift and terrible as Duvalier unleashed his Tonton Macoutes on the mulatto stronghold of Jérémie. The militia was ordered to terrorize the city. Hundreds were killed and many mulatto families were massacred. In the fourteen years of Duvalier's rule the political and cultural influence of the mulatto elite was significantly eroded.

Since the nineteenth century the mulatto elite has been pro-French and Catholic. They developed a version of Haitian history that saw the true heroes as Ogé and Chavannes and according to which Presidents Pétion and Boyer were the true fathers of Haitian independence. Consequently, they saw theories of race and a return to Africa as a retreat from civilization. The prejudiced nature of the Haitian elite prompted the observation that "many of them say that the Negro can never originate a civilization and that with the best of education he remains an inferior man, utterly unfitted for government, utterly incapable of making progress."[2]

They were equally suspicious of leftist theories, which invariably attacked their commercial interests in Haiti. Given Haiti's history, it seems ironic that there is little trace of resentment among the elite against France, which had enslaved Haitians and against which a terrible war had to be fought for independence. The lure of France remained largely unchanged. As was further observed, "The more time the elite spend in France, the less kinship they feel with the masses. There is not necessarily any conscious snobbery in this increasing discrepancy; it simply results from a life spent in entirely different environments."[3] Although they professed a higher level of culture and enlightened political principles, this did not prevent the elite from defending an authoritarian approach to politics and putting class interests above everything else.

The elite has often been dismissed as that tiny percentage of the population that does not work with its hands, and under Francois Duvalier they paid a terrible price for their political cynicism and cultural superciliousness. Many have felt that the solution to Haiti's social and political problems lay in the creation of a middle class. This was particularly true during the occupation, when U.S. policy makers felt that one way of guaranteeing stability for Haiti was through encouraging the growth of a middle class through new educational opportunities such as vocational training. The access of this group to state power and patronage began under Estimé's presidency. It also played a crucial role in Duvalier's ability to govern because it supported his noiriste politics and his anti-elite policies. The Episcopal or Anglican Church has been strongly promoted by this emergent class, which has been seen as an answer to the problem of social mobility in Haiti. Its existence, it was thought, might be the key to liberal democracy and the modernization of Haiti. This belief exists even more strongly today because such a class is seen as the only way of eliminating the pseudo-serfdom that has marked Haiti's class division. A recent sympathetic account of contemporary Haitian society noted that

> If you cast your eyes wider than the palace grounds, you can see dozens of small churches, with their paper flowers hanging behind the altar, and their broken fans, their makeshift seating arrangements and slatted windows. Besides the Macoutes and the police and the Army, there are the car salesmen, the dry cleaners, the jewelry storeowners, and the poor relations who work for free in the homes of their wealthier aunts or uncles or cousins.[4]

This view "beyond the palace grounds" suggests the teeming world of an urban middle and lower middle class that is very different from the tightly knit group of families that constituted the traditional urban elite.

No treatment of the urban elite can be complete without mention of the Syrian and Lebanese community (referred to generically within Haiti as Syrian). By the 1880s Levantine immigrants had arrived in sufficient numbers and had become sufficiently successful in business for there to be fierce anti-Arab feeling in Haiti. By the turn of the century there were an estimated 2,000 of them involved in the import trade, with close ties to their counterparts elsewhere, especially in the United States. The resentment toward these recent immigrants came as much from market women whose livelihood they threatened as well as from wealthier businessmen involved in the import-export trade. Pressure was put on governments at the turn of the century to limit their activities, and often nationalist politicians threatened to expel them from the country. Because of such attacks, many did leave Haiti in the early twentieth century. Those who stayed on became very rooted in Haitian society and their numbers grew during the U.S. occupation. They were generally scorned as nouveaux riches by the mulatto elite. Although they were never active in Haitian politics, they supported Duvalier's regime, and at various times members of the Arab community served as ministers in Duvalier's government. Because of their minority status there has always been a close bond among members of this community. Their businesses are also usually family run. As the traditional elite came under attack, they began to emerge as the business elite of Haiti and continue to retain that status today. The decline of France as a major influence in Haiti and the close links with the U.S. have also enhanced the status of the Syrian and Lebanese business community.

The Haitian elite today is essentially a business elite, made up of several dozen families of which the most important at the present time are the Mevs and the Brandts. They continue to play a monopolistic role in the Haitian economy. This oligarchy runs its businesses in the old-fashioned way, with minimum investment and absolute control over certain sectors of the economy like the light assembly industry, textiles, and coffee and sugar production. These families that dominate the private sector took strong opposition to the sweeping social reforms attempted by Aristide's Lavalas movement. They resisted any attempt to redistribute the wealth of Haiti and even declared the law to raise the minimum wage to be "anti-national." They most of all feared Aristide's encouragement of the militant grassroots organizations, trade union groups, and peasant cooperatives. They were much happier with dictatorships that suppressed opposition and are said to have played a key role in financing the coup d'état that overthrew Aristide's government in 1991.

THE PEASANTRY

The dramatic development of distinctive cultural patterns in Haiti not only created, as we have noted, a cosmopolitan, urban elite culture but also was responsible for the emergence of an ostracized and exploited peasantry, which became the base of an economic system in which available arable land became increasingly scarce and methods of production stagnated. Shortly after the abandonment of the plantation system, a peasant society emerged whose existence was based on small plots of land. As the population rapidly grew, so did this sector of society, which is made up of 70 percent of the population in one of the most densely populated countries in this hemisphere. This peasantry is accurately described by the Haitian Creole expression *moun andeyo* ("people on the outside") and as profits from peasant labor were increasingly siphoned off to support a minority of the population, the peasantry was destined for abject poverty.

The world of the Haitian peasantry has remained substantially unchanged for the last two centuries. They still live in tiny thatch-roofed huts (*cailles*), without light or water, outside the towns, where illiteracy is rampant and healthcare and sanitation are rudimentary at best. An accurate description of this world is that

Haiti is probably the only country in this Hemisphere where neither the plough nor the wheelbarrow is generally used. Crop rotation is unknown. Congo peas, millet (piti mi) or yams are grown over and over again on the same hillside until a very low yield forces the peasant to burn off and move nearby; when nature and cattle grazing restore some fertility, he returns to the original plot.[5]

Typical Haitian peasant villages consist of a dozen or so huts grouped together on remote mountainsides where members of a large extended family live. This kind of arrangements is called the *lakou* and is essential to the organization of collective labor, or *coumbite*, which is still used for work in the fields. The food crops grown, in addition to those mentioned by Rodman, are maize, rice, red beans and manioc (tapioca). The most frequently grown cash crops are coffee and rice in the Artibonite valley, even though the typical form of agriculture practiced is subsistence farming. The typical *lakou* would also contain a few chickens, pigs, and a donkey, or *bourrique*, for transport.

The world of the Haitian peasant is an isolated communal one. Through the family, individuals are socialized and learn the rules that must be followed. Religion forms part of this need for cohesion and collective identity. Such units do not resist state aggression but find ways to avoid or ignore the state, since contact with it always poses a threat to the equilibrium of the peasant's world. Such inward-looking behavior traits can have both negative and positive effects. They may explain why anything that is seen as coming from the outside is deemed intrusive and is eroded by peasant mistrust; thus development projects are left to decay as soon as the foreign experts are gone. These tightly knit communities are also responsible for such traditions as the *coumbite*, or communal labor, a West African tradition that allows the peasant farmer to perform major agricultural tasks that he is unable to do on his own. The regular sharing of labor in each other's fields is one of the more positive aspects of peasant solidarity.

The Haitian population contains more women than men, and in peasant society women play an important role. As many observers have noted, the peasant woman's life is totally different from that of her elite counterpart. Hers is a life of unremitting labor. Weddings are infrequent in the Haitian countryside; common-law arrangements, or *placages*, dominate, despite the assiduous efforts of the Catholic Church to eradicate them. The number of wives that one man may have is determined by land holdings. Not only do women share in such laborious tasks like tilling the fields, they are responsible for child care and food preparation. Most important, they are responsible for selling surplus produce in the numerous rural markets and for buying various items like medicine, kerosene, and household articles that the peasantry cannot produce for itself. One of the most common sights in the Haitian countryside is an endless line of women coming from the hills balancing enormous loads on their heads or riding donkeys with loaded baskets.

Women are important intermediaries between the peasant villages and the markets and towns. The market, the main outlet for peasant produce, is dominated by women. On the way to the market, they run the risk of being robbed by soldiers or taxed by local authorities until the margin of profit on their goods has practically disappeared. At the market, they can spend all day in the sun and sleep nearby at night. It has even been written that "babies are born frequently in the market place, the mother having come down from the hills only that day to sell her goods."[6] Quite often, the peasants sell their goods to female retailers, or *revendeuses*, who travel across the countryside buying goods that can be resold at a profit. These women, also nicknamed "Madam Sara" after a noisy local bird, are an essential part of Haiti's rural economy. In recent times they have become more generalized hagglers, sometimes traveling outside the country to acquire goods for resale.

The hundreds of rural markets in Haiti—with their bustling confusion, teeming with women and children, and their mixture of smells—are a crucial aspect of Haiti's rural economy. Equally important is the income the peasant makes from the sale of cash crops, especially coffee, which plays a significant role in the Haitian economy. Unlike the marketing of surplus produce, the sale of cash crops is outside the peasant's control: it is organized by an export marketing system dominated by the elite. Coffee is the favored crop of the peasant farmer, but unfortunately for the peasantry it has also been the main source of government revenue. The fee and taxes placed on coffee for export are invariably borne by the peasant farmer. Whenever the government increases its levy on coffee, the families of the elite, which control the commodity, simply pass the extra costs down to the middlemen, or *speculateurs*, who in turn pay the farmer less for his produce. The peasant farmer has no choice but to accept the price offered to him, since the coffee trade is tightly controlled by the members of the oligarchy, who control the export of coffee.

Land is another problematic issue in rural Haiti, both because of the destruction of the environment and the complicated business of land tenure. Even though the war of independence had ruined Haiti's infrastructure, the land was still fertile. Poor farming techniques and ignorance of soil conservation have, over time, ruined the environment. Trees have been cut down to provide lumber, charcoal, and clearings for cultivation in an overpopulated countryside where every available acre is put to use. The frantic search for arable land has led the peasant farmer into the forested interior of Haiti. This has meant that the land was 98 percent forested at the time of Columbus is now only 9 percent forested. Seventy percent of Haiti's energy is supplied from charcoal. Incredibly, charcoal was being exported until recently to other

Caribbean islands. In some areas of the country, particularly the northwest, this situation has created desertlike conditions and famine.

One reason for deforestation is the issue of land tenure and over-population. As the land is divided into smaller and smaller plots—usually because land owned by a family is divided into an ever greater number of heirs, but also simply because of the combination of an increasing population and decreasing arable land—the plots that are farmed are barely viable. On such plots the farmer is unlikely to surrender precious soil to growing trees. Also, quite often a peasant farmer may own a widely dispersed number of tiny plots that are farmed by landless peasants. This creates a situation where the peasant farming the land has no interest in long-term environmental questions. Leaving trees standing in such circumstances becomes a luxury.

Until recently, the peasant in this condition of abject poverty and complete neglect by the state has been a docile conformist creature, dedicated to little more than his individual plot of land. The absence of official titles and the subdivision of land because of inheritance have also made the peasantry vulnerable to predatory state officials. Under Duvalier, many Tonton Macoutes and section chiefs used this state of confusion to expropriate peasant land. This vulnerability to outside forces was once more apparent in the 1980s with the slaughter of the pig population by the U.S. Agency for International Development. Not only did this eradication exercise further impoverish the peasant, the promised compensation rarely materialized, largely because of corruption. The vulnerability of Haiti's rural sector to tragic abuse became apparent in 1987 when 4,000 tons of toxic waste from Philadelphia were dumped in the port of Gonaïves by a U.S. cargo boat. The potential contamination from this waste is yet to be determined, and no legal attempt has been made to pursue the local officials who were involved in this massive threat to the environment.

With the spread of desertification, famine and drought have become realities in the rural sector, which faces its greatest threat ever. It is generally understood that any radical change in Haiti must involve the transformation of the Haitian peasantry. The question has been how to transform people who see themselves as passive victims or who live in isolated, self-sufficient enclaves into politically conscious agents of social change. For many observers, the closed, creolophone world of the peasantry prevents them from fully grasping the tragedy of their lives. "This uncomplaining acceptance of life, routine, and fate seems to be the essence of peasant existence. The Haitian peasant has been bound to the soil by mental inertia and by tradition more effectively than ever by law."[7] The fall of Jean Claude Duvalier in 1986 was preceded by rural unrest, which suggests precisely such a transformation of peasant society. Part of the explanation for this change from passive acceptance to activist confrontation is tied to the media and the use of radio and cassettes as important forms of communication. However, even more important than the media in bringing about such changes was the activism of an institution that is normally closely linked to the elite: the Catholic Church.

In the 1970s, a significant number of Haiti's indigenous clergy and committed lay people, encouraged by inspired by the ideal of social justice and developing political awareness of the poor, created a grassroots movement called the Ti Legliz ("little church"), which preached social justice and human rights for all. The mobilization of the peasantry was achieved through what were essentially training centers scattered outside the capital and devoted to leadership training. Ti Legliz concentrated on the training of *animate* (community leaders) in such areas as literacy, civic education, and agricultural extension services. Indeed, this level of mobilization ensured that, after the fall of Duvalier in 1986, the peasantry would no longer be the silent majority. The Ti Legliz first showed its capacity to mobilize the peasantry in the overwhelming vote for the new Haitian constitution in the summer of 1987. The second manifestation of the power of the grassroots Catholic Church was in the presidential elections of 1990, which brought Aristide to power. The day after he announced his candidacy, voter registration shot up massively, indicating the effects of increased political awareness among the peasantry. This experience may have changed Haitian peasants definitively. No longer at the mercy of middlemen and a predatory military, they show signs of a new autonomy and self-confidence, they have greater control over their livelihood. One of the oldest and most effective of the peasant movements is the Papaye Peasant Movement in the Central Plateau, whose main aim is to give peasants control over production. *The New York Times* could, as a result, carry a story in 1995 of Haiti's peasant farmers that observed,

> With the grain speculators who once controlled prices no longer able to call on armed bands of enforcers, it is finally safe to begin storing crops until the price rises. . . . [A]ssociation members are already talking about building four more silos, rebuilding their credit fund so that they can buy more crops, and learning more sophisticated growing techniques.[8]

The most important national events in Haiti have traditionally been preceded by unrest in the countryside. The politicization of the Haitian peasantry may be the most important factor in Haiti's transition to a more just and democratic society.

THE URBAN POOR

Because of the blatant social divisions in Haiti, there has been a justifiable tendency to emphasize just two sectors of a very divided society. However, to do so in too categorical a fashion would be to misconstrue the internal dynamic of an economic system that does involve some measure of contact with urban centers. For some time there has been persistent contact between peasant and town dweller: "In the nineteenth century, as now, the distribution of agricultural products depended on weekly or seasonal trips by members of the peasantry into the urban areas. . . . Through such daily or seasonal to-and-fro, repeated for generations, the peasants mounted the ramparts of the cities."[9]

This analysis suggests that, although it was isolated from political and economic power, the Haitian peasantry was nevertheless exposed in varying degrees to the outside society and to elements of Westernization. This contact became more persistent and desperate with the dramatic decline in productivity in the agricultural sector and the migration of the peasantry to the towns in order to find work and shelter.

The rural sector in Haiti had always been plagued by a number of major problems, but by the 1980s agricultural production for local consumption as well as for export plummeted. The accelerating decline in agriculture posed as much a problem for the rural sector as for central government, which derived much of its revenue from duties on exports. This economic crisis was compounded by the negative publicity from the belief that the AIDS virus was endemic in Haiti, which destroyed the tourist industry. The deteriorating economy meant the worsening of the plight of the two thirds of the population that lives in the countryside. With no social services, no hospitals, and no schools, the average annual income by the end of the 1980s had dropped to less than $100. This crisis provoked an exodus to the towns on a massive scale. For instance, the population of the capital, Port-au-Prince, estimated at about 500,000 in the 1970s, grew to well over a million by the end of the 1980s.

These refugees from the countryside are drawn to the towns because of work. However, there are few jobs for the uneducated and unskilled. In any case, to get a job would require contacts among the influential. Few of the new urban poor enjoy any such privilege. Therefore, they find themselves employed intermittently as laborers and cart pullers (known as *bouretyes*) or in repairing shoes, bicycles, or motor cars. Relatively few, mostly women, have found themselves employment in the light assembly sector, where they earn no more than the minimum wage. In the impoverished human chaos of the urban slums, there are two manifestations of this human tragedy that are striking: street children and the phenomenon of the *restavek*. A 1993 UNICEF report estimated that there were approximately 2,000 street children in Port-au-Prince who survive by various forms of begging, theft, and prostitution. Many of these children may have begun as *restaveks*—that is, children sent to the towns to work as unpaid servants for less impoverished family members. The rural families believe that the children will be better off in the towns. However, invariably the children are mistreated, overworked, and not paid. They continue in this miserable state until they become eighteen and then, quite often, street people.

As a result of this demographic crisis, Haiti's major towns and its capital have become spectacular scenes of squalor and deprivation. Even if social services, health, and education were marginally better in the towns, they have now collapsed under the pressure of this influx of the rural poor. Port-au-Prince, in particular, epitomizes urban chaos with its improvised street markets, unending traffic jams, and run-down infrastructure. Spectacular slums, or *quartiers populaires*, now encircle Port-au-Prince. These shantytowns, with ludicrous names like Brooklyn and Miami, mushroom on the outskirts of the city in areas like Carrefour and La Saline, on the seafront. In these areas, thousands of people live in cramped wooden or block houses covered by zinc sheets. These are the lucky ones, as the less fortunate must make do with sheets of plastic or cardboard. One of the poorest areas is called Cité Carton (Cardboard City) because dry carton boxes are used as construction material.

The most notorious of Haiti's slums is Cité Soleil, to the north of Port-au-Prince. This area, which began as a low-income housing project on swampy land near the coast, was soon taken over by squatters. It now houses about 400,000 people crammed together without any of the basic amenities like water, electricity, or sanitation. For most of these slum dwellers, the only source of water is a public well or standpipe. Water is available only late at night and early in the morning. It is therefore not uncommon to see girls and women balancing plastic buckets on their heads in the dark, labyrinthine streets of these shantytowns. Equally noticeable are the massive piles of garbage that remain oozing in the tropical heat. Occasionally, attempts are made to incinerate these massive piles of refuse, but the fires can hardly prevail against the pile-up of trash, and they simply add to the prevailing stench.

What makes Cité Soleil one of the worst slums in the world is its location just above sea level. During the rainy season, there is no protection from the downpour, and the water, filled with floating garbage, rises quickly in the stifling rooms where an average of eight persons sleep and eat. Rooms usually have only one bed, which sleeps a minimum of four adults. People sleep in shifts and walk around the neighborhood when awake, which explains the teeming nature of these slums at all hours of the night or day. Those who are less fortunate are obliged to sleep standing up, leaning on walls.

Much of the power of Haiti's priest-turned-politician, Jean Bertrand Aristide, can be explained by his relationship to the dispossessed of Cité Soleil, which was once part of his parish. These areas also became the scene of a new kind of street-level politics as militant neighborhood committees were formed in the wake of Duvalier's departure. They became the driving force behind *dechoukaj*, the need to uproot the vestiges of Duvalierism from the society. The urban poor represent a force capable of challenging the elite-dominated society of Haiti. Because of the urgent need to change their desperate situation, they are spurred to violent protest and demonstrations, even against those members of the Lavalas movement who are seen as obstacles to change.

THE DIASPORA

In our examination of the urban poor we have been looking at a phenomenon created by internal migration from rural to urban areas. However, when people think of Haiti, it is not this kind of migration or refugee that comes to mind; external migration has made Haitians most visible to the outside world. This is especially the case since the 1970s with the increasing exodus of Haiti's rural poor across the sea to Florida. This pattern of migration was exacerbated in the 1990s as Haitians fleeing political persecution as much as economic hardship left their homeland in thousands and created a major human-rights crisis. These migrants have been disparagingly called "boat people" by the international media. The roots of Haitian migration and migrant communities go much deeper than this recent dramatic manifestation of the phenomenon and have much to do with Haiti's political and economic interaction with the outside world.

Whenever Haiti's isolation from the outside world has been breached, there almost inevitably follows a pattern of migration. For instance, the U.S. occupation of Haiti and massive U.S. economic investment in the sugar industry in the neighboring countries of Cuba and the Dominican Republic at the beginning of the twentieth century led to the acute need for cheap labor to harvest the sugar cane. The significance of this phenomenon is evident in the well-known Haitian novel *Gouverneurs de la rosée* (Masters of the Dew), in which the main character is a cane cutter who comes to Haiti from the plantations in Cuba. With sugar prices rising because of World War I, the need for labor intensified, and by 1920 the number of Haitian workers in Cuba had reached 36,000. This migratory pattern was fueled by rural dislocation in Haiti as attempts were made by U.S. investors during the occupation and afterward to create a plantation economy in Haiti. Such schemes inevitably led to the expropriation of peasant land and increased the willingness of the peasants to seek their fortunes overseas.

Migration to the Dominican Republic has similar roots but is profoundly influenced by the suspicion and hostility that has marked the relations between the two countries. As in the Cuban case, Haitian migration to the Dominican Republic was linked to the rapid expansion of the sugar industry during the U.S. occupation of the Dominican Republic from 1916 to 1925. By the 1930s, Haitian cane cutters had begun to take up permanent residence on the eastern side of the border. This illegal settlement of Haitian immigrants was used by the Dominican dictator Raphael Trujillo in his nationalist campaign to encourage anti-Haitian feeling. In 1937, at least a quarter of the 50,000 Haitians living in the Dominican Republic were massacred by Trujillo's troops. Despite this tragic event, Haitians have continued to migrate to the Dominican Republic, driven invariably by their desperate economic plight. In a very short space of time the number of Haitians massacred was replaced by new waves of migration. Despite the inhospitable nature of the Dominican Republic and the overtly racist attitudes of the Trujillo and later Balaguer regimes, the number of Haitian immigrants settled there was roughly estimated at half a million in 1990.

Because of their illegal status and the ever-present threat of deportation, Haitian workers are paid badly and are always subject to forcible mass repatriation. For instance, in 1991 President Balaguer ordered the deportation of some 8,000 Haitian cane cutters, or *braceros*, in response to the criticism of the treatment of Haitian workers by President Aristide. The plight of the *braceros* became a major international issue in the 1980s when a French journalist wrote a graphic story on life in the plantation compounds, or *bateyes*. The slavery-like conditions described in the story were confirmed by a delegation from the International Labor Organization, which substantiated the poor working conditions, the use of child labor, and the use of the Dominican military to keep the workers imprisoned on the *bateye*. However, the problem of exploitation by the Dominicans is complicated both by the Haitian workers' desperation for jobs and the corruption of Dominican and Haitian officials. In the hope of earning quick money, Haitian workers are crossing the Dominican border illegally even as their compatriots are being expelled. This illegal migration also invariably occurs under the eye of corrupt Dominican officials. Haitian recruiters are also paid to transport the workers to the Dominican plantations.

It is estimated that 16,000 workers are needed to harvest sugar cane. Despite the fact that unemployment in the Dominican Republic is estimated at 30 percent, the Dominicans shun the low wages and the harsh working conditions in the fields. There has never been an agreement regulating the use of migrant Haitian labor in the Dominican Republic. The election of President Leonel Fernandez promised improvement and the establishment of a treaty between both countries. There is still no such treaty, but a commission now oversees the contracting process at the border. Due to increased pressure from international organizations, the Dominican government has begun attempting to give some kind of official status to children of Haitian families born in the Dominican Republic. However, this recruitment of Haitians is resented by Dominicans who feel that there are already too many in the country illegally. Even as the hiring of new workers continues, the Dominican army expels Haitians by the hundreds in an apparently arbitrary manner. The possibility of a return to power of President Balaguer in forthcoming elections does not augur well for Haitian-Dominican relations.

A slightly different type of migration from Haiti has occurred since World War II. Although migration to the Dominican Republic is largely by foot and the migrants are impoverished rural folk, this second phase of migration to other parts of the Caribbean is not from the worst-off sections of the population. These migrants are invariably farmers, fishermen, or market women who can afford the cost of the passage to Caribbean destinations like the Bahamas and to a lesser extent, the French departments of Guadeloupe and French Guyana. Whereas the French authorities grant the Haitian migrants permits to work primarily in the sugar and banana industries, in the Bahamas the rapid expansion of the tourism industry in the 1960s created employment opportunities for Haitian immigrants.

No one is sure of the number of Haitians who have settled in the Bahamas, since most of them are illegal and their dependents are undocumented. It is estimated that there are as many as 40,000 Haitians in the Bahamas, which is equal to almost a quarter of the total population of the Bahama Islands. As is generally the case, the well-paid jobs went to the Bahamians, thereby creating a need for workers who would perform various kinds of manual labor and menial jobs. Therefore, large numbers of Haitians could find employment in construction and as gardeners and servants. Since the vast majority are illegal immigrants, they can be compelled by their employers to work for low wages. The Haitians also face enormous difficulties in the Bahamas because of their lack of skills and training and also because of their illiteracy and their inability to communicate in English. The fate of Haitians in the Bahamas is a precarious one; they are periodically rounded up by immigration authorities and deported to Haiti. The effect of migration to the Bahamas is particularly noticeable in the northwest of Haiti, which is often affected by drought. Remittances from Haitians in the Bahamas have a positive effect on the economy of this impoverished section of Haiti.

HAITIANS IN NORTH AMERICA

North America has become in recent times the principal target for Haitian migration. At first, large-scale migration to North America began in the late 1950s and was made up of skilled and professional Haitians seeking a better life abroad. This brain drain began in earnest with repression under the Duvalier dictatorship. In the face of harassment by the state, many lawyers, doctors, teachers, and engineers took their skills to places like New York and Montreal. An often-repeated statistic illustrates the point most graphically: of the 264 medical graduates of the School of Medicine in Port au Prince, only three remained in Haiti. Haitians are fond of observing ruefully that there are now more Haitian doctors in Montreal, Canada, than there are in Haiti.

Since this initial exodus of professionals, all classes of Haitians have settled in North America. For example, there is a significant community of Haitians in Miami in an area christened Little Haiti, and there are an estimated 250,000 Haitians resident in New York. In some parts of New York, particularly Brooklyn, Creole is widely spoken and many businesses are owned by Haitians. There is less and less of a sense of uprootedness from the native land and a greater feeling of easy continuity between Port-au-Prince and Brooklyn. Haitians in the United States even have their own weekly newspapers, *Haiti Observateur, Haiti en Marche*, and *Haiti Progrès*, which publish articles in French, Creole, and English. Much of the Haitian economy is made up of remittances sent home by these migrants, and this gives the latter enormous influence at home. Quite often, after establishing themselves in New York, these immigrants have brought in other family members to join them. As is to be expected, class divisions characteristic of Haiti are reproduced abroad. For instance, poorer Haitians settle in areas of New York that are distinct from districts settled by the upper classes. Language is also important in establishing class divisions. For instance, because of the social stigma attached to Creole, upper-class and light-skinned Haitians insist on using French as a tool for achieving social mobility in the United States. It is also a way of escaping an identity as a racial minority in the United States and a way of distinguishing themselves from African Americans.

A second phase of migration to the United States was inaugurated in 1972, when the first boatload of Haitians arrived in Florida. This meant that poorer Haitians, who could not afford visas and airfares, were able to buy a seat on these boats by selling their possessions and leave for the 700-mile trip to Florida. This was the beginning of the Haitian "boat people" phenomenon, which grew in intensity because of the intensifying economic crisis that plagued the regime of Jean Claude Duvalier. This pattern of illegal migration to the United States grew to such an extent that there were almost a thousand illegal Haitians arriving in Florida each month. American authorities concluded an agreement with the Duvalier regime in 1981 allowing the Coast Guard to intercept the Haitian boat people at sea and forcibly repatriate them. For the next few years thousands of Haitians were repatriated and no one is sure how many were lost at sea because of the crowded and leaking boats or because of being thrown overboard by unscrupulous boat owners.

Despite the abysmal human rights record of the Duvalier regime, these migrants were considered economic and not political refugees and therefore not entitled to asylum in the United States. The situation, however, became more complicated after the 1991 military coup that ousted Haiti's first democratically elected president. In the chaotic aftermath of President Aristide's ouster and the brutal repression that followed, thousands fled Haiti by boat because of a well-founded fear of persecution. Nevertheless, President Bush used the 1981 agreement to order the forcible repatriation of Haitians intercepted at sea in May 1992. Even though President Clinton promised to change this policy, Haitian boat people were never granted refugee status, in stark contrast to their Cuban counterparts. In mid-1994, the waves of Haitian boat people threatened to overwhelm the resources of the U.S. Coast Guard, and the United States was forced to create a holding camp in Guantanamo. The specter of a massive exodus of impoverished black Haitians to the shores of Florida may ultimately have been the single most important factor in the deployment of U.S. troops to Haiti to dislodge the de facto military regime and reinstate constitutional rule, thereby making the case for political asylum untenable.

The Haitian American diaspora is now said to number one million; it is commonly viewed as the "tenth department," as Haiti itself is divided into nine administrative regions, or departments. Despite the strong links maintained with their native land and their tendency to see their stay in the United States as temporary, very few members of the tenth department have returned to settle in Haiti. The growing realization that the transition to democratic rule in Haiti is likely to be a long and chaotic process has made many Haitian Americans feel that they can serve their motherland better by agitating for the Haitian cause in the United States. The first signs of this new political activism could be seen in 1990 when thousands of Haitians marched in New York City to protest the official designation of Haitians as a high-risk group for the AIDS virus. The stigma that resulted from such a designation could have lead to the ostracism of all Haitians regardless of class and color. The solidarity and victory achieved by this march, as the U.S. government eventually reversed its position on Haitians and AIDS, have done much to unify Haitians abroad.

This display of solidarity would later be repeated as members of the tenth department marched through Manhattan in 1991 to protest U.S. inaction toward the military coup that overthrew the Aristide government. This growing capacity for political mobilization is one of the more positive consequences of Haitian migration. Haitian American businessmen now join the political race for the Florida state house and for seats in the state legislature. Efforts are being made to organize candidate forums and mobilize the Haitian vote so that Haitians can become a force in American ethnic politics. This new activism means a political coming of age for Haitians in North America. A new generation of politically astute and well-educated Haitian Americans is attempting to influence U.S. policy on Haitian issues. A new generation of Haitians who arrived in the United States as children have now become adults and enjoy an unprecedented commercial success. The painter Jean Michel Basquiat, the rap artist Wyclef Jean, and the novelist Edwidge Danticat are some of the more dramatic examples of the new mood of self-confidence among Haitian Americans and their increased involvement in their country of adoption.

Whereas an older generation of Haitian immigrants in North America was, in general, more defensively nationalistic, staunchly anti-Duvalierist, and obsessed with political intrigue in Haiti, a younger generation of Haitian Americans is now more concerned with events in the adopted country and lives a dual heritage more fully. There has been some tension between these two generations, who were formed at different times and in different cultures. The old guard feels that the newer generation is inauthentic and insufficiently attuned to the traditions and politics of the native land. The younger generation wishes to break with what it sees as the folkloric stereotypes of the past and to project a modern identity as Haitian Americans. Tensions between these two factions in the Haitian community abroad became apparent in 1997, when protests were organized against police brutality because of the alleged police beating and torture of a young Haitian, Abner Louima, by the New York police. On August 29 the younger generation of Haitians in the United States organized a protest march in Manhattan through their association, the Haitian American Alliance, which attracted about 10,000 people. A similar march organized two weeks earlier by the old guard attracted merely 2,000 protesters. The difference in the numbers attending these marches suggests important shifts in allegiance in the Haitian American community. Despite the fact that they are condemned by older Haitians as naive upstarts, the second generation of Haitians in North America is a force to be reckoned with. The following description of members of the Haitian American Alliance by *The New York Times* is very telling and points to a new image of Haitians in North America:

> The Haitian American Alliance has about 80 members, including a coterie of thirty something doctors, lawyers, accountants, teachers and artists, many of whom were born in the United States. Many have attended some of this country's best schools and share a fondness for sushi as well as rice and beans, the Haitian staple. Their musical tastes range from the Haitian pop star Sweet Mickey to the American jazz musician Wynton Marsalis.[10]

This picture stands in sharp contrast to an older generation that migrated from Haiti in the 1960s during the dictatorship of Francois Duvalier and has ever since been obsessed with overthrowing that regime. This sense of mission has been undermined by the fact that the Duvaliers are no longer in power and by the need for a new kind of leadership with new ideas. The Louima incident brought the Haitian American Alliance to prominence and signals the emergence of a new image of Haitians that may well represent a definitive break with the old stereotypes of rural poverty and bloody dictatorship. One of the most visible signs of the new image of Haitians in North America was the crowning of a Haitian American as Miss America in September 1990. This event, perhaps even more than economic performance and political activism, reveals the extent of Haitian integration in the United States.

NOTES

1. James Leyburn, *The Haitian People*, rev. ed. (New Haven, CT: Yale University Press, 1966), 101.

2. Ibid., 107–108.

3. Ibid., 110.

4. Amy Wilentz, *The Rainy Season: Haiti Since Duvalier* (New York: Touchstone, 1989), 399.

5. Selden Rodman, *Haiti: The Black Republic* (New York: Devin Adair, 1954), 36.

6. Leyburn, *The Haitian People*, 197.

7. Ibid., 108.

8. Larry Rohter, "Rooting Up Fears: Haitian Farmers Fill the Silos," *New York Times*, February 3, 1995. Online.

9. Michel Rolph Trouillot, *Haiti, State Against Nation: The Origins and Legacy of Duvalierism* (New York: Monthly Review Press, 1990), 82.

10. Gary Pierre Pierre, "For Haitians, Leadership Split Is a Generation Gap," *New York Times*, September 24, 1997. Online.

3

Religion

WHENEVER the question of religion in Haiti is raised, it is invariably answered by the popular saying that Haiti is 90 percent Catholic and 100 percent vaudou. The paradox of the religious situation in Haiti is that even if there is a wide gap between rich and poor and even if the official religion of the state is Roman Catholicism, the practice of vaudou is not only pervasive but interchangeable with Catholicism. Despite the fact that the elite disapproves of vaudou and is hypersensitive to the tendency among foreigners to see Haiti as the country of vaudou, the fact is that the vast majority of both the rural and urban population are vaudou worshipers. The situation is further complicated by the fact that although the masses are practitioners of vaudou, they are likewise Roman Catholics. The only exceptions to this tangle of religious practices are the Protestants, who might account for 10 percent of the population and who seem less prone to practicing vaudou than members of the more ritualistic Catholic faith.

Another general feature concerning religious practice in Haiti that should be noted is the relationship between church and state. From the very outset, the struggle for independence tied religion to politics in Haitian history. For example, the vaudou religion, an amalgam of West African religious beliefs that was widely practiced on the plantations of colonial St. Domingue, provided a means of retaining a link to the past and establishing solidarity and communication among the slaves. The Catholic Church in the colony, on the other hand, did little to make the treatment of the slaves less brutal. It is therefore not surprising that vaudou played an important role in slave revolts in Haiti, such as the revolt of Makandal in the mid-eighteenth century and the ceremony in the Bois Caiman held by Boukman on the eve of the Haitian revolution. Nor should it come as a surprise that the Catholic religion was viewed as the religion of colonial oppression and would be accorded no special status after independence. Indeed, Dessalines prescribed no official religion in his constitution; he both granted freedom to all religions and denied state support for any particular one. This separation of state and religion, however, did not favor the religion of the Haitian masses. Vaudou was viewed with suspicion by Dessalines and Toussaint before him. They both saw it as a potential center of opposition and as an embarrassment in a world where Haiti was constantly accused of lapsing into savagery.

After Dessalines' assassination in 1806, Catholicism was adopted as the official religion of Haiti in Pétion's constitution and by Christophe in the north. Later, the francophile Boyer in particular was strongly in favor of not only the Catholic religion but of establishing formal ties with the Vatican. This would not come to pass until many years later, but Boyer's regime did establish a particular coziness between the Catholic Church and the Haitian state and entrenched the view that vaudou was nothing but a dangerous superstition. This led to an inevitable alignment between the mulatto elite and the Catholic Church. It would also mean that vaudou would tend to be championed by nationalist ideologies seeking to establish culturally authentic practices in Haiti and dislodge the francophile elite. There is consequently a consistent pattern of rejection of Catholicism by nationalist or noiriste presidents such as Soulouque and Duvalier, who was actually excommunicated by the Vatican. It was also partly in reaction to the excesses of Soulouque's regime that Geffrard signed the Concordat with the Vatican in 1860, allowing the Church to play an increasingly important role in the country and to ultimately reinforce mulatto hegemony.

The fact that the principal schools in Haiti were run by religious orders and were staffed by French priests reinforced the francophile attitudes of the educated and encouraged prejudices against the religion of the masses. After having been the religion of the colonizer, Catholicism became profoundly associated with a neocolonial mulatto elite and defined as an unprogressive vestige of the colonial past. The strongest argument against Catholicism was first explicitly made by the essayist and nationalist Louis Joseph Janvier. Janvier saw the Concordat of 1860 as a threat to Haiti's sovereignty and as a surrender of Haitian culture to the control of the mulatto elite. Janvier's anticlerical position would be repeated again and again by nationalist intellectuals. The idea of giving official state support to a foreign religion, which was staffed by priests from Brittany in France and controlled from Rome, was seen as abhorrent by those who thought that the sacrifices made for Haitian independence meant precisely the end of this kind of foreign influence. The concordat with the Vatican allowed the Catholic Church to practically create an autonomous state within the Haitian state.

Janvier's arguments against Catholicism were also broader in scope. He felt that the religion was deeply prejudiced against the black race. Not only had Catholicism sanctioned the enslavement of blacks, it was opposed to the development of a local clergy, preferring to import foreign priests instead. Janvier not only reiterated the charge of racism against the Catholic Church but also accused it of being profoundly antimodern. He felt this religion was hostile to economic development and favored too mystical and ritualistic an attitude to life. In this regard, Janvier distinguished himself from other ultranationalists because he did not turn to the vaudou religion as an alternative to Catholicism. Though acknowledging the important role of vaudou in the struggle for independence, Janvier felt that vaudou's usefulness was now spent and that another kind of religion was needed to modernize Haiti. He sought a solution in Protestantism, which he thought encouraged pragmatism and self-reliance and was furthermore more suited to what he saw as Haiti's African temperament. Protestantism could also be aligned more closely with the social and economic objectives of the Haitian state. In his appropriately named *Haïti aux Haïtiens* (Haiti for Haitians) published in 1884, Janvier set out the factors that complicated relations between religion and politics in Haiti and that would ensure continual friction between church and state in Haiti.

This friction led to open hostility during the U.S. occupation, which reestablished mulatto dominance in political life in Haiti. The Catholic Church was accused by the militant nationalists at the time of collaborating with the Americans and of waging a campaign against the culture of the masses, in particular the vaudou religion. For example, two of the major writers of the occupation years, Carl Brouard and Jacques Roumain, were strident in their criticism of Catholicism. Brouard championed a mystical approach to vaudou, which made it more suited to the Haitian psyche and made Catholicism into a form of spiritual alienation. The Marxist ideologue, Roumain, who was opposed to Brouard, shared the latter's hostility to Catholicism. He adhered to a doctrinaire approach to Marxism and saw Catholicism as perpetuating a subservient and colonial mentality among a rural peasantry that needed to be liberated from an archaic mentality. The religious populism that was pervasive among radical Haitian intellectuals in the occupation period and after was often countered by mulatto intellectuals such as Dantes Bellegarde and Stenio Vincent, who argued strongly and predictably for the Catholic Church's involvement in Haiti and denounced vaudou as a an embarrassment to the civilized world and as the main cause of Haiti's backwardness.

The conflict between the defenders of Catholicism and of vaudou became particularly bitter in the early 1940s because of the Catholic Church's campaign against vaudou, which was conducted with the support of the mulatto then-president, Elie Lescot. Lescot declared, soon after his election in 1941, his government's support for Catholicism. This was seen as explicit support for the Catholic Church's campaign to rid Haiti of what was called the cult of Satan. The excesses of this campaign waged by foreign priests against Haitian peasants and their religious culture created great controversy at the time. In particular, it was seen as a desperate attempt by the mulatto elite to hold onto power in the face of increasing challenges from black middle- and working-class opposition groups in Haiti. The collapse of the Catholic Church's campaign against vaudou in 1942 was seen as an early victory for a pro-vaudou nationalist opposition that would dominate Haitian politics after Francois Duvalier became president.

By the time Duvalier came to power in 1957, there was a widespread view that Haiti needed to have an indigenous clergy. It was also noticed that the Episcopal Church in Haiti was far less hostile to vaudou than the Catholic Church. Indeed, in order to celebrate the bicentenary of Port-au-Prince in 1949, the Anglican bishop of Holy Trinity Cathedral, an American, commissioned a number of Haitian primitive artists to decorate the interior of his cathedral. By 1959 Duvalier's prolonged battle with the Catholic Church manifested itself. He saw the Roman Catholic hierarchy as a potential center of opposition to his regime, but he viewed the Episcopalian Church as an ally and a key link with U.S. interests. Duvalier's reaction to Catholicism can be traced back to Janvier's earlier critique of Catholicism as a threat to sovereignty. Duvalier differed from the 19th-century essayist in his defense of vaudou as an authentic religion and one that allowed him to even more effectively control the Haitian peasantry.

In 1959 there began a series of expulsions of Catholic priests from Haiti, a purge of the education system, and the official banning of the Catholic newspaper *La Phalange* in 1961. A year later the papal nuncio (Vatican representative to a civil government) was recalled to Rome and all involved in what the Catholic Church called "the violation of its sacrosanct rights" were excommunicated. By 1965, the power of the Catholic Church in Haiti was broken and Duvalier pressed for a basically indigenous clergy to be introduced into Haiti. The Vatican agreed to this compromise, and in 1966 Duvalier finally had what he wanted: an education system under the control of a local clergy that was expected to give support to the state's policies. A clear example of the Catholic Church's docility was its willingness to perform the marriage ceremony between the divorced Michele Bennett and Jean Claude Duvalier.

Ironically, it is this very indigenous clergy that brought about the demise of Jean Claude Duvalier in 1986. This came about because the indigenization of the Haitian clergy meant that, with vaudou intimately associated with the Duvalier dictatorship, young grassroots elements in the Catholic Church became extremely influential in the impoverished countryside and the urban slums. Many of these priests who saw themselves as members of the Ti Legliz, or grassroots church, were influenced by Liberation Theology, a militant political movement started in the Catholic Church in Latin America. These priests also distinguished themselves from the members of the high clergy and the council of archbishops in the Catholic Church in Haiti. By the time Pope John Paul II visited Haiti in 1983, thousands of Ti Legliz groups, or C.E.B. (*communautés écclesiales de base*), had been established across Haiti. The pope's call for things to change in Haiti gave further authority and confidence to this grassroots movement, which emerged in the forefront of the anti-Duvalier opposition movement.

This radical element in Catholicism gave organizational support to the revolution for change by providing the structures for political discussion and action. As the *houngans*, or vaudou priests, showed some reluctance to join in the anti-Duvalier riots in the early 1980s, the Ti Legliz grew in moral stature among the poor. Indeed, it would not be an exaggeration to compare this grassroots movement in Haiti with the other Church-supported displays of people power elsewhere in the world such as in the Philippines, the Middle East, Eastern Europe, and Latin America. The drama that was being played out in the 1980s in Haiti turned on the emergence of tensions between an unarmed majority demanding radical social and economic changes and the complicity of a radical wing of the Church, which had for too long blessed the rich and the powerful in Haiti. In Haiti's northern town of Cap-Haïtien, for example, the Church's role was particularly evident. The cathedral was often used as a rallying point for demonstrators, and the local religious radio station became the voice of the movement. On one memorable occasion, this station, Radio Ave Maria, broadcast a recording of the pope's message to Haiti and encouraged all its listeners to turn up the volume on their individual sets in a gesture of defiance. Such a concerted demonstration of solidarity fostered the feeling that the people's rebellion was legitimate and that the Church was behind the objectives of the people's struggle.

The absence of political leadership meant that the Ti Legliz assumed an unprecedented role in Haitian society. This role in politicizing the Haitian masses was further enhanced by the Catholic radio stations, which were particularly effective in a country where the vast majority of the population is illiterate. The best known of these religious stations is Radio Soleil, which acquired such a reputation that after the departure of Jean Claude Duvalier the most populous section of Port au Prince was renamed Cité Soleil in honor of the station's radical activism during the opposition to Duvalier. Like so many other religious stations, Radio Soleil, formed in 1978, was created both to spread the Gospel and improve literacy. However, this station became the most popular in Haiti and quickly changed its programming to Creole, including sermons from radical priests reporting human rights abuses and interviews with ordinary Haitians.

The power of the Ti Legliz and conflict with the conservative council of archbishops became even more apparent in the period following Duvalier's exile. The mobilization of the Haitian masses to vote for the revised constitution in 1987 is largely the work of politicized Church groups throughout Haiti. The emergence of Jean Bertrand Aristide as a national leader is also an obvious consequence of the activist role of the Ti Legliz. Another clear consequence of the activist Church's success is the increase in the number of young Haitians entering seminaries to train for the priesthood. It is also evident that the popular resentment of the Church hierarchy and the Vatican is justly related to two factors: the fact that archbishops have never enthusiastically endorsed radical change in Haiti, and the close association of certain leading Church figures with the Duvalier regime. Resentment has also been directed against well-known *houngans* because of their refusal to associate themselves with the anti-Duvalier movement. This chain of events has resulted in a new role for the religion in radical politics in Haiti. It has also left the Ti Legliz in a position of uncontested strength and Jean Bertrand Aristide, a former Catholic priest, as the only national leader to emerge in post-Duvalier Haiti.

CATHOLICISM

Given the testimony of many visitors to colonial St. Domingue that self-indulgence, immorality, and cruelty to the slaves were the order of the day, it seems safe to say that religious obligations were never held in high regard in Haiti before independence. The planters treated the Church with indifference. Priests who showed some interest in saving the souls of the slaves were seen as subversive. In fact, the Jesuits were expelled for precisely this reason in the late eighteenth century. The priests who stayed on in Haiti were not overzealous in their duties. The free mulatto *gens de couleur* were reported to be as irreligious as the French planters. The slaves themselves, deprived of religious instruction, clearly saw vaudou as the religion through which they channeled their hopes for freedom.

The protracted war of independence put religion at an even lower ebb. After the revolt of 1791, Catholic priests fled or went into hiding with the white planters. Toussaint did make an effort to rehabilitate the Church because he saw it as a stabilizing institution. However, neither was post-revolutionary France particularly interested in promoting religion, nor were French priests willing to make their way to a country where there had been black insurrection. The violence that brought Haiti to independence in 1804 further marginalized spiritual matters. The precarious nature of the Catholic Church in Haiti was intensified with the open schism that existed between the Vatican and the new Haitian state. Rome refused to either recognize the fledgling state or allow priests to enter Haiti. Early Haitian leaders were never openly hostile to the Catholic Church, but formal relations were not established with the Vatican until 1860.

The absence of a properly functioning Catholic Church in these early decades meant that people grew away from the doctrines and practices of a religion that never really had much of a presence in pre-independence Haiti. Even if early leaders favored Catholicism as the official religion, the head of the Church was inevitably the president. During Boyer's long presidency, in which Catholicism was particularly promoted, there were only seventy priests in Haiti, some of whom were defrocked or little more than religious adventurers. The status of the Catholic Church fell to an all-time low during Soulouque's presidency. In the 1840s vaudou flourished with official approval, and the state allowed whatever little status was reserved for Catholicism to disappear. The reaction against Soulouque's excesses made the justification for adopting Catholicism relatively simple. The best time to promote Catholicism would obviously be after an embarrassing period in which vaudou was openly practiced. Negotiations with Rome began as soon as the new president came to office in 1859. With the Concordat of 1860 and the conservation of a Catholic archbishop in Port au Prince the schism of fifty-six years was ended.

It was, however, too late to rehabilitate a religion that had never gained a foothold in Haiti during the formative years. By 1860 vaudou had become firmly entrenched in the Haitian countryside and in the popular culture as a whole. Even the elite, despite its ostensible rejection of vaudou, practiced it clandestinely. The situation was complicated by the fact that the native religion had incorporated elements of Catholicism, and so to practice vaudou did not necessarily mean the denial of Catholicism. There were simply two interchangeable theologies and divinities, each with its own powers and rituals, in the minds of most Haitians. Consequently, what the new Catholic priests encountered in 1860 was not hostility or rejection but an ineradicable native religion that had grafted itself onto Catholicism and retained all the outward manifestations of Catholicism.

The archbishop of Port-au-Prince and his small band of forty or so priests set about reconstructing Church buildings that had become derelict. One of the most imposing buildings today in the largely nondescript capital is a pink and white stone cathedral begun in 1884 and finished in 1915. Similarly, in the north, the aluminum metal domes of the cathedral tower above the largely ramshackle city center.

Haiti was divided into dioceses named after its principal cities. Thus, there are the archdioceses of Cap-Haïtien and Port-au-Prince and the dioceses of Hinche, Jérémie, Jacmel, Cayes, Gonaïves, and Port-de-Paix. The country's 10,200 square miles are further divided into parishes that generally correspond to political communes. In remote rural areas, mission chapels are strategically located. The majority of Catholic brothers in Haiti belong to the Frères de l'Instruction Chrétienne. These Breton priests established the prestigious secondary school, St. Louis de Gonzague, in Haiti's capital city. It contains the best library in Haiti today. They also have jurisdiction over a number of elementary schools. The Fathers of the Holy Ghost, a priestly order, established an important center of higher education known as the College de St. Martial, also called the Petit Séminaire. The Catholic sisters belong to three orders: St. Joseph de Cluny, Les Filles de la Sagesse, and Les Filles de Marie. The nuns of St. Joseph de Cluny operate a large high school for girls, and the sisters of La Sagesse manage a number of hospitals.

Until the 1950s there was no Catholic seminary in Haiti. Duvalier, in his bid to indigenize the clergy, invited Canada-based Jesuits to establish a national seminary in Haiti. Because of this convention enacted with the Jesuits, Catholic priests in Haiti today also come from Quebec, Canada. In 1966 Duvalier achieved victory in his fight with the Vatican, and a protocol was signed allowing for the nationalization of the Haitian clergy. Duvalier invoked a rule that existed in the Concordat of 1860 that gave Haitian presidents the right to appoint bishops and archbishops, pending the Vatican's approval. This right had never been previously exercised. Duvalier, however, reclaimed the privilege and supervised the consecration of a number of new Haitian bishops. With his usual skill in dismantling sources of opposition, Duvalier had co-opted the Catholic Church; its compliance with Duvalierism would be its undoing after the Duvalier regime collapsed.

The Catholic Church in Haiti is, to all appearances, well established, but until the emergence of the Ti Legliz it was difficult to tell the extent to which its teachings influenced the lives of most Haitians. Even if by assiduous teaching brothers and sisters managed to acquaint the peasants with religious forms and beliefs, they were never able to make them believe exclusively in the Catholic faith. The masses saw no difficulty in attending a vaudou ceremony on Saturday night and going to Mass on Sunday morning. Furthermore, a *prêt savan*, or bush priest, often officiated in vaudou ceremonies, reading the Pater Noster and the Ave Maria from a prayer book. The altar, the crucifix, holy candles, and saints' images are invariably present during vaudou rituals. The Church apparently had a greater effect on the upper classes, whose children went to school. The elite were also shrewdly using the religion to establish class differences by distancing themselves from vaudou. They also felt that by practicing Catholicism they could gain the approval of the outside world.

The Catholic Church's lack of effectiveness among the majority was also tied to its prejudice against the Creole language. For the longest while, the Mass was celebrated in languages unknown to the majority of Haitians: Latin for the rituals and French for the sermons. It is consequently difficult to assess the impact such a service would have on the Creole-speaking masses. The elite outwardly professed Catholicism, and it has always been considered proper to attend church. However, no loss of prestige results from not attending church services. Assiduous displays of religious devotion are also sometimes used to counter charges that an individual is a practitioner of vaudou. Furthermore, the color and class divisions in the society were for too long reflected in the Church, where black priests were considered, even by the peasants at times, as unfit for administering the sacraments. The reaction against masses in Creole is another example of the elite's snobbishness penetrating the Catholic Church, "For the elite, well groomed, sitting . . . in a seat bearing his nameplate, the psychic elation to be derived from hearing a sermon preached in a language which the rabble . . . does not know must be very great—and very Christian."[1]

Roman Catholicism is the officially approved and socially accepted religion, but its presence in Haiti is intricately tied up with the folk religion. Perhaps the most dramatic illustration of this relationship between superstition and religion in Haiti and of the problematic attitude to vaudou in the Catholic Church can be found in the miraculous appearance of the Virgin Mary in the tiny village of Ville Bonheur in the rugged mountains of central Haiti in 1884. She is supposed to have appeared in a palm tree and remained long enough for the whole countryside to witness this apparition. The parish priest felt this was mere local superstition and came to drive the Virgin away.

She left, but people kept coming to the spot by the palm tree where she had been seen and were miraculously cured or helped in their moment of need. The priest tried to stop this practice by attempting to chop down the tree but was wounded by his own machete. Eventually, the tree disappeared and the Church tried to take advantage of this phenomenon by erecting a church on the supposedly sacred spot. It was, however, destroyed by fire, as was each successive church building erected there. The Virgin next appeared during the U.S. occupation. Legend has it that a local priest tried to get rid of it by having an American marine fire at the apparition. The marine complied and the apparition left, but the priest's house was destroyed by fire and within a week the priest died.

The Catholic Church rather grudgingly recognized the apparition, and the miraculous event was thenceforth celebrated annually, with a full day of religious observances every July 15. Thus, after attempting to combat the sanctity of the event, the Church then tried rather clumsily to co-opt it. However, the pilgrimage to this shrine, situated by a waterfall called Saut d'Eau, close to the base of the palm tree, is undeniably vaudou in character. Small plates of food are frequently left alongside the votive candles at the Virgin's shrine, and the pilgrims are often mounted by the *loa* (vaudou deity) when they bathe in the waterfall. The Virgin had clearly become identified in the popular imagination with Erzulie, the primary female *loa*. Once again the popular imagination had prevailed and altered the meaning of a ceremony that the Church wished to identify as Catholic. The display of mysticism by the pilgrims at Saut d'Eau seems more like a vaudou ceremony than any remotely Catholic rite to one observer:

> The waterfall at Saut d'Eau carves a deep hidden basin from a limestone escarpment, and by the time I arrived shortly after midnight the entire vault was bathed in the soft glow of a thousand candles. Already in the depths where no moonlight could fall, huddled together, or darting in and out of the water, singing the vaudou songs or serving the many altars, were dozens and dozens of pilgrims. On all sides, people saturated with a lifetime of heat shivered and trembled, drawing in their hands against their naked skin.[2]

Catholicism in Haiti got a new lease on life with the emergence of the Ti Legliz in the 1980s. However, deep suspicion of the radicalism of grassroots priests by the Vatican and the conservative nature of the Catholic archbishops, many of whom were appointed with the approval of the Duvalier regime, meant that followers of the Ti Legliz saw the Catholic hierarchy as hostile to their interests. This mistrust of the high clergy began soon after 1986, when the Council of Bishops reacted against the violence aimed at former Macoutes by denouncing the process of *dechoukaj* (uprooting vestiges of Duvalierism), probably out of fear that they too might fall victim to this process. In their sermons the bishops seemed more concerned with denouncing the violence of *dechoukaj* than with the question of justice at the end of twenty-nine years of a brutal dictatorship. The Catholic Church may have been irrevocably damaged by the hierarchy's attempt to rein in the Ti Legliz by abandoning the Mission Alpha literacy program and transferring popular grassroots priests from their parishes.

To this day, relations between the official Catholic Church and the majority of Haitians are poisoned by the sustained efforts of the Vatican to silence Father Aristide. The antagonism between Aristide, then a parish priest in the Salesian order, and the papal nuncio, Archbishop Ligondé of Port-au-Prince, who was related by marriage to the Duvaliers, was not lost on the followers of the charismatic priest. The decision to have Aristide removed from his church at St. John Bosco was seen as just another strategy to undermine the people's movement. Increasingly, the Catholic Church found itself yet again in league with the Haitian army and the political status quo. After a siege of the cathedral in the capital and a hunger strike by Aristide's more militant young parishioners, the bishops were forced to give in to the parishioners' demands that Aristide not be moved from St. John Bosco. The massacre of parishioners during mass at Aristide's church, and the burning of the building afterward, further confirmed in the minds of many the Church's desire to eliminate the most influential member of the Ti Legliz. In 1989, the weapon of last resort was used against Aristide: he was expelled from the Salesian order. From that time on, Aristide became confirmed in the popular imagination as a prophet; the politicizing of the Ti Legliz into the Lavalas movement had begun, and the nuncio and the Council of Bishops were seen as the incarnation of evil.

PROTESTANTISM

It is very difficult to establish the impact of Protestant religions in Haiti. Their presence was so precarious in 1941 that one sociologist declared in his study of the Haitian people, "No Protestant sect has ever gained a foothold in Haiti."[3] However, Protestant missions have since become increasingly active in Haiti, and the number of Haitians said to belong to Protestant churches ranges from 10 to 20 percent of the population. Part of the problem in assessing the presence of Protestantism is the variety of denominations active in Haiti. Among the major Protestant churches are the Anglicans, Methodists, Seventh-Day Adventists, Jehovah's Witnesses, and Baptists. Smaller, more fundamentalist denominations like the Mennonites and Mormons also maintain missions in Haiti. They operate schools, hospitals, and various kinds of workshops, and vocational training facilities. One of the largest centers for higher education in Port au Prince is the College Bird, which is run by the Methodist Church. Protestants also run the radio station Radio Lumière. Their attitude to vaudou is not uniform: the Episcopalian and Methodist Churches have been more flexible in this regard than some of the more rigidly fundamentalist sects. They are all, however, viewed with suspicion by the Catholic Church, which sees them as favoring radical politics or U.S. interests and thereby weakening the French advantage in Haiti.

One way of understanding the influence of Protestantism in Haiti is to divide the denominations into two groups. On the one hand there are those churches that established themselves in the nineteenth century, of which the Anglicans and the Methodists are the most important. On the other hand, there are those far more numerous and more recent churches, which are overwhelmingly North American and have been very successful in gaining converts in the Haitian countryside. They gained a foothold after the U.S. occupation; the largest of these is the Haiti Baptist Mission. The older Protestant churches established themselves in the towns and grew slowly because of the domination of urban religious and educational institutions by the Roman Catholic Church. The more recent evangelical and fundamentalist sects have gained their converts in the impoverished rural areas, where Catholicism is less entrenched and where conversion is invariably tied to handouts in the form of food or clothing.

Except for the mainstream Protestant churches, no overarching hierarchy unites the various Protestant congregations. In general, their disparate and scattered presence in Haiti is a reflection of the schismatic heritage of American evangelicals. Apparently it is not difficult for independent Protestant missions in Haiti to find financial sponsorship in fundamentalist parent churches in the United States. These evangelical missions have grown enormously since the 1960s, when they flourished because of increasing hardship in the countryside. The Duvalier regime tended to have a laissez faire policy toward these fundamentalist sects, which were seen as a harmless form of foreign aid. They served Duvalier's interests well since they were strongly apolitical, opposed to radical social change, and took care of the material needs of remote rural communities.

Protestantism first officially came to Haiti in 1817 when then President Alexandre Pétion invited the abolitionist John Brown and others to come to

Haiti. Thus, early Protestantism was seen as progressive and a requiem mass was ordered for John Brown when he was executed in 1859 for his raid on the U.S. Arsenal at Harper's Ferry, West Virginia. The earlier permanent Protestant church in Haiti was the Wesleyan church, a branch of Methodism. In 1861, under President Geffrard, African Americans were encouraged to migrate to Haiti to escape racism at home and to aid the Haitian economy This scheme, promoted in the United States by the abolitionist James Redpath, brought to Haiti more than a hundred African Americans, one of whom was the Reverend James Theodore Holly. He set up the Episcopalian, or Anglican, Church in Haiti and in 1874 became the first bishop of the Eglise Orthodoxe Apostolique Haïtienne. He established branches of the church elsewhere and continued his religious work until his death in 1911.

The building of the Anglican Saint Trinity cathedral was completed in 1928 by the Reverend Harry Roberts, who had been ordained the first missionary bishop to Haiti in 1923. He was succeeded by another American, Bishop Alfred Voegeli from New Jersey, who was responsible for the decoration of the cathedral walls by Haitian primitive artists. In general the Anglicans had no problems with training local priests nor with the use of the Creole language and local music in the church services. The church's budget is funded mostly by contribution from the United States. In general, these more mainstream Protestant churches have not been hostile to social change and to preserving the folk traditions of Haiti. The Methodist Church has been very involved in adult literacy and rural rehabilitation programs since the 1960s. The prestige of Protestantism increased during President Aristide's exile because of the support he received from the Reverend Jesse Jackson and black Protestant churches. It was even rumored at one point that President Aristide might himself become a member of one of the Protestant churches.

The trend towards indigenization of clergy and the role of Protestantism in literacy campaigns in Creole have ensured a positive reaction to mainstream Protestant churches among nationalist thinkers in Haiti. Janvier, in criticizing the Concordat of 1860, felt that Haiti was more suited to Protestantism, which was infinitely superior to Catholicism because it offered incentives for development and democracy. Since then this faith has often been advanced as a solution to the modernization of the Haitian masses. The strong emphasis on Bible study and conversion by rational choice in Haitian Protestantism has also guaranteed its involvement in literacy campaigns. It is, therefore, not surprising that the image of mainstream Protestant churches has not suffered since the fall of Duvalierism. One popular and outspoken candidate for the presidency was Sylvio Claude, a Protestant minister. The head of the first and much embattled electoral council that was formed to

organize elections after Duvalier's 1986 departure was the Methodist pastor
Alain Rocourt.

More recent and more fundamentalist missions from the United States
have been viewed more suspiciously, with some justification. Fundamentalist
missionaries invariably regard vaudou as the religion of Satan and the chief
cause of Haiti's backwardness. Conversion to these faiths means the explicit
rejection of vaudou. These missionaries also harbor strong prejudices against
peasant culture as a whole and are suspected of simply indoctrinating their
converts into an amorphous dependency on handouts from North America.
Conversion is often related less to a genuine crisis of conscience than to a
pragmatic desire for self-betterment. Instead of making the dangerous trip
to Florida in a leaky boat, the converted peasant can attain certain basic
economic aspirations within a church. One account of the proliferation of
these conservative sects in Haiti and in particular of the Baptist Mission of
the white Southern preacher Wallace Turnbull, known locally as Pastor
Wally, is revealing:

> All along Route Nationale, everywhere you go, you see Protestant Mis-
> sions: Mission Possible, H.E.L.P., Mission to Haiti, Inc., Larry Jones
> Hands of God Ministries, hundreds of others. The most famous and
> perhaps the most grandiose of all is the Baptist Haiti Mission up above
> Boutilliers, at Fermathe . . . Haiti has not done badly by Pastor Wally.
> At the mission, he presides over some two hundred and fifty Haitians
> who call him "Bos," and who rake and hoe and harvest and sew in
> return for clothing and religious schooling and care from the small but
> clean medical clinic. To work at the mission you must be baptized. In
> general, Pastor Wally does not pay his workers, he feeds them, usually
> with food from CARE's Food for Work program.[4]

There has been inevitable conflict between reactionary sects such as that
of Pastor Wallace's mission and the Ti Legliz with its peasant cooperatives.
Feelings are particularly intense when it comes to the issue of food cultivation
and the dependency created by evangelical sects on handouts of American
food aid. The issue came to a head in 1987 when in Jean Rabel, in the north
west of Haiti, militant peasant farmers from the Tet Ansanm cooperative
were massacred by Duvalierist landowners because of conflicts over land
tenure. In this area, which suffers from desertlike conditions and the serf-
dom of the sharecropper system, grassroots Catholics clashed with former
Macoutes who had been instigated largely by a tract published and distributed by Pastor Wallace. This circular portrayed the peasant movement

as "communist," which served perfectly the interests of the Duvalierist families who had traditionally controlled the area. Jean Rabel is just the kind of destitute area that is likely to become the recipient of the charity of the evangelical missions. It is also an area where the Ti Legliz has managed to counter the gospel of resignation with a new dynamism among the peasantry. The confrontation between grassroots Catholicism and conservative Protestantism in rural Haiti brings a new twist to the complex religious situation that has always existed in that country.

VAUDOU

Vaudou is the word used to designate popular religion in Haiti. It is a Afro-Haitian religion with a system of beliefs that explain the links between natural and supernatural worlds. For the elite, vaudou is an embarrassment. The various established churches in Haiti anxiously await its demise. It has been embraced since the 1920s as Haiti's true culture by radical intellectuals. The only Haitian president who gave it a special place of honor in his regime ruthlessly exploited it to remain in power. The grassroots Ti Legliz movement has all but eclipsed vaudou in recent times. In the period of violent *dechoukaj* that followed 1986, hundreds of vaudou priests were denounced as supporters of Duvalierism and killed. Yet vaudou stubbornly persists, hardly changed from the early days of the Haitian nation. Conservative in nature, led by priests who are at best half literate, vaudou knows neither formal orthodoxy nor monotheistic creed, nor is it averse to borrowing liberally from the rituals of a church that has sworn to destroy it.

The role that vaudou has played in Haitian history remains elusive and ill defined. Militant nationalists have perhaps exaggerated its importance in the war of independence against the French. Despite the importance of the Bois Caiman ceremony, it would have been impossible for Boukman to emerge as head of a widespread organization because vaudou has always consisted of a number of small *societés* and could never be manipulated by one individual. The early leaders of independent Haiti—Toussaint, Dessalines, and Christophe—distrusted vaudou because of its elusiveness and its ability to create disorder. Until relations with the Vatican were formalized, vaudou was allowed to develop unimpeded as a nationwide religion for what had emerged as Haitian peasant society. While Catholicism languished and the state was involved in political struggles, the Haitian people gained access to land and established their culture and religion in the countryside. Therefore, the first half of the nineteenth century in Haiti saw the emergence of vaudou as the people's religion in Haiti.

The question of vaudou's influence on the Haitian state before Duvalier is uncertain. Even in the Duvalierist state, Papa Doc deliberately maintained ambiguous relations with a religion that he knew inspired fear but in which he did not himself believe. Foreigners took special pleasure in depicting Haitians as demonic cult worshipers. Vaudou became the source of lurid reports of cannibalism after the Affaire de Bizoton in 1863, when eight Haitians were executed after the killing of a young girl in a ritual sacrifice. The trial aroused much publicity, and subsequently a number of tales were spun of fiendish practices related to folk religion. This practice intensified after the United States occupied Haiti in 1915. In particular, vaudou was linked to zombification because of William Seabrook's sensationalist travel book, *The Magic Island* (1929). Hollywood soon followed with films like *The White Zombie* (1932) and, more recently, Wes Craven's *The Serpent and the Rainbow* in 1988.

Many Haitian commentators, on the other hand, after vigorously denying vandou's importance in national life in the nineteenth century, may have idealized it out of all proportion in the wave of nationalism associated with the indigenous movement. The work of Jean Price-Mars, the subsequent interest in ethnology in the 1930s, and the establishment of the Bureau d'Ethnologie in Port-au-Prince in 1944 did much to provide objective scientific accounts of various aspects of the vaudou religion. Anthropological studies by Melville Herskovits, Harold Courlander, and Alfred Metraux in the 1930s and 1940s also provided much of what we know today about the vaudou religion and its role in peasant life. Since the 1940s, however, vaudou has increasingly become part of an exotic tourist industry for the titillation of jaded locals and foreigners alike. This commercialism of vaudou was particularly apparent during the regime of Paul Magloire (1950–1956), when the tourist trade with the United States flourished. This kind of commercial exploitation would inevitably have had an effect on a religion that was originally the belief system of the Haitian masses. One author notes with some dismay the degrading effect of tourism on Haitian vaudou:

> Many *hungan* [vaudou priests] and *mambo* [vaudou priestesses], who for several years have been pleased to see parties of Americans turn up at their *humfo* [temple], have responded with alacrity to the curiosity of foreign clients. The *humfo* threw open wide their doors to the tourists; link-ups were made between hotel porters and *hungan* to such good effect that on Saturday evenings long files of cars may be seen in some wretched back street near a sanctuary. Some enterprising *hungan* have even put on Voodoo "shows" which are repeated weekly and designed

purely for tourists. . . . Sanctuaries have become neon-lighted theatres. Great sums may have been made by the *hungan* and *mambo*, but they have driven away the true believers from their temples.[5]

Vaudou is the religion of the Haitian countryside, where the overwhelming majority of Haitians still live. The extent to which it persists in cities is tied to the individual's attachment to his or her rural roots. Before the revolution there is little evidence that the white planters took vaudou seriously. It seems to have been dismissed by some as harmless superstition and by others as an incomprehensible nocturnal diversion. Given the control and domination of the slaves' lives and freedom of movement by the plantation, it was only in the area of spirituality that slaves had the capacity to express themselves. Since even the most rigid plantation owners allowed drumming and dancing, the dance became the ritual around which a slave religion was formed. Vaudou ultimately emerged as a product of the various cultures and religious practices of slaves brought from West Africa from the sixteenth to the eighteenth centuries. The most prominent group of slaves were Dahomean in origin. Their numerical superiority ensured that Dahomean practices would be dominant in the new religion created by the slaves. Vaudou became a systematic set of beliefs and practice by 1791 and acted as a unifying force during the war of independence, making communication possible across barriers of language and culture among the slaves.

The word *vaudou* is, not surprisingly, Dahomean in origin, as are many of the characteristics of vaudou theology. The various deities of this religion are called *loas* or sometimes the French word *mystères* is used. The term *vaudou* is used to designate the beliefs and rituals of this religion. Vaudou theology is divided into a complex polytheistic system of spirits over which one all-powerful god dominates. This Supreme Being, or *le bon Dieu* (the good God), has all the characteristics of the Christian concept of God. However, this god is seen as too distant and impersonal to pay attention to the needs of ordinary Haitians. This fatalistic attitude to god means that He, along with Jesus Christ, the Virgin Mary, and the Saints, is relegated to the background of the spiritual life of the peasantry. The attention of the adepts of vaudou is therefore monopolized by the pantheon of *loas*, whose worship and appeasement are the essential function of vaudou.

The vaudou pantheon is not standardized and is always being increased as ancestors or even priests can become *loa* after their death. However, there are two dominant systems of belief, each with its own practices and deities. They are the *rada* rites (named after the town of Arada in Dahomey) and the *petro* rituals. These two groups are called *nanchon*, or nations, and each one has its own rhythms, instruments, dances, and invocations. The origin of the *loa* is fundamental to their classification into nations. The *rada* nation is made up of deities that are Dahomean or Nigerian in origin. While there are many African-derived deities (and even some of the *rada* spirits are repeated) in the *petro* group, the majority are Creole in origin and are more recent additions to the vaudou pantheon. The basic difference between the two nations is related to the fact that the *petro* spirits are more violent and unpredictable. The *rada* group is more gentle and do not inspire fear. The *petro* spirits are the *loas* of last resort. When all else fails or when the devotee wishes to turn to sorcery, the *petro loas* are invoked. It would be an exaggeration to brand all the *petro* spirits as evil, but it is true to say that many are called "devils" or "eaters of men."

The *loas* are said to live in Guinea, a mythical place without specific geographical location. They leave this vaudou version of heaven and come down to earth when they are invoked. They can frequent certain streams, mountains, or caves. They are also present in trees, and each *loa* has his or her favorite kind of tree. These sacred trees or resting places, which were especially targeted during the anti-superstitious campaign of 1941, can be recognized by candles burning at their roots or by food left beside them. Each *loa* has one or two days a week considered sacred to him or her. Each *loa* also has a preferred color. Vaudou does not have an extensive mythology attached to it, and what we know of the gods is concretely manifested when a devotee is possessed by a particular god. The possessed imitate the walk, the voice, and the mannerisms of the spirits, which have been made manifest. The spirits can, and often do, inflict supernatural punishment on those who have in one way or another offended them. Various ailments and persistent bad luck are attributed to the gods, and madness is always explained as a divine punishment. The *loas*, if sufficiently offended, can visit the sins of parents on their children. Someone who has lost the protection of the *loas* is considered very vulnerable and is often beset by a sense of helplessness.

The profusion of spirits in Haiti makes any list of *loas* necessarily incomplete. However, there are some principal deities that are commonly invoked. In any list of vaudou *loas*, the first place goes to a god of Dahomean origin, Legba. He is the most frequently invoked because he is the interlocutor between the gods and man. He guards the crossroads or the gateway. If he is not invoked first there is no access to the other gods. Therefore, care must be taken not to offend him. He is affectionately addressed as "Papa Legba" and often associated with the Catholic St. Anthony. He is represented as a lame old man who moves about painfully with the help of crutches, a haversack slung across his shoulder. Nevertheless, his role as the mystical barrier that divides gods and men is a crucial one in the vaudou pantheon. His pitiful appearance conceals his tremendous power, which can become apparent in the violent trances that are induced when an individual is possessed by him.

Erzulie, or Erzuli-Freda-Dahomey, is the most important and most frequently invoked female *loa*. She is a combination of Aphrodite and the Virgin Mary and her symbol is a heart pierced by a sword. She is often portrayed as light-skinned and is the personification of feminine grace and beauty. In every vaudou temple there is a corner devoted to this deity with red and blue dresses, jewelry, perfume, and various cosmetics. She can possess either male or a female. The possessed person is dressed extravagantly, and Erzulie makes her appearance in her full seductive glory, ogling the male devotees and swinging her hips. She has a scandalous reputation among the gods. She does not have as specific a function as Legba. As a *rada* deity, she can be approached without fear. In her *petro* manifestation, she is called Erzulie-Je-Rouge, or red-eyed, and she can be boisterous and violent.

Damballah, the serpent god, was once thought to be the most important of the spirits. Since his symbol is the serpent, which is viewed as diabolical by the Christian faith, Damballah has been seen as evidence of satanic worship among the Haitian peasants. This is by no means the case. He is associated with the Catholic St. Patrick and with the sign of the rainbow. He is invariably depicted with his wife, Aida-Wedo, as two entwined snakes. Anyone possessed by him hisses and makes sinuous movements, climbing trees or the supports of the vaudou temple. The rainbow and wealth are associated in Haitian mythology, and Damballah can permit a treasure to be discovered. All trees are natural resting places for Damballah, but he is also considered an aquatic deity, haunting springs and rivers.

Along with these three major deities are numerous other *loa*s, among whom a few stand out. The *loa* who presides over the elements is also extremely important in the vaudou pantheon; his name is Agoue and his realm is the sea. All creatures that live therein as well as those who live off the sea come under his jurisdiction. He is also the protector of seafaring Haitians, not the least of whom are today's refugees. His emblem is a miniature boat, and like all sea deities his color is white. Agoue is light-skinned with sea-green eyes and is invariably dressed in a naval uniform. He is worshiped near the sea or a river. Sometimes a special service in his honor is held on a boat decorated with vaudou flags and streamers. Ritual sacrifices are thrown into the sea, and care must be taken so that the possessed do not jump overboard.

Another major spirit is Ogun, who is derived from the Yoruba people of Nigeria. He is the god of war and thunder. His color is red and he is said to protect those who serve him from being wounded by weapons. Ogun is always depicted waving a saber and is associated with St. James. There is also a possibly even more fearful group of spirits, related to death, funerals, and cemeteries. These are the *guedes*, and their most fearsome representative is Baron Samedi. They express themselves in a very nasal voice and are closely associated with obscene language, gestures, and an erotic dance called *banda*. They are dressed in dark veils, top hats, and frock coats. A pair of dark glasses is indispensable. They can come disguised as corpses with cotton in their mouths and nostrils. Baron Samedi, the most disturbing of the *guedes*, has a black cross as his emblem as well as a skull and crossbones. His wife, who also has dominion over the cemetery, is Gran Brigitte. The image of the *guedes*, and Baron Samedi in particular, was exploited by Duvalier in the way he dressed and by the Tonton Macoutes' in their predilection for dark glasses.

The dead are as important as the *loa*s as a category of supernatural beings. Funeral ceremonies are complex procedures that mix Christian and vaudou rites. One of the most important rituals related to burial is the removal of the *loa* who has protected the individual during his or her lifetime. This ceremony of *desunin*, or the breaking of the bonds with the spirit world, must take place immediately after death and must be conducted by a vaudou priest. The dead are buried without hat or shoes, and their pockets turned inside out to sever all contact with the world of the living. The deathwatch, or wake, is a mixture of the sacred and the profane, of sadness and joy, as card games are played alongside the expression of heartrending lamentations for the dead individual. The most important aspect of the funeral and burial is the need to disorient the dead and prevent them from returning to haunt the living. The perpetual threat of the dead person's return preoccupies family members during the period of mourning. Novenas (Catholic prayer rites) are held to propitiate the dead, and black clothes must be worn by the mourners if the dead are to rest comfortably

In order to understand how the spirits are invoked and how possession takes place, a clear idea of the vaudou sanctuary is necessary. The sanctuary is called a *hounfor*, and each one is independent. These sanctuaries are not, strictly speaking, temples. Quite often they are little more than religious centers that can be recognized by the peristyle, a colonnade or covered area where ceremonies and rituals are performed. The corrugated iron or thatched roof of the peristyle is held up by gaudily painted supports, of which the middle one is called the *poteau-mitan*. This is literally a central sacred feature of the *hounfor*; around this post dances are performed, and down it the gods descend. There is little to suggest that the sanctuary is a particularly sacred place or one that houses spectacular displays of spirit possession. The sick are sometimes housed there, and it can be used as a place for a number of household chores, like ironing and shelling peas. The peristyle is usually adjacent to the room, or *baji*, where the altar is found. The *baji* contains all the necessary articles for vaudou rituals: clothes, objects, sacred jars, Baron Samedi's hat, and Legba's crutches, for instance.

The vaudou priest is called a *houngan*, or papa-loa, and the vaudou priestess is called a *mambo*, or mama-loa. A priest who is adept at magic and sorcery is called a *bocor*. To take the *asson*, or sacred rattle, is to become initiated as a priest. The priests are considered to be people who have found favor with the *loa* and have acquired a special *connaissance*, or knowledge. The priest is as much a teacher as a healer or a fortuneteller, and his or her role is to bring a concrete manifestation to the mysteries of the religion. The priestly role is not even limited to the realm of the spiritual: priests can give advice on political matters or be village counselors. In the religious hierarchy, the second in command in the *hounfor* (temple) is the *laplace*, the priest's chief assistant. Those who are initiated and regularly assist the *houngan* during the ceremonies are called the *hounsi*, or wives of the gods. They are mainly (but not always) women and are sworn to the worship of the spirits. They fulfill all the domestic chores that come with being spouses of the gods, and they must be prepared to spend nights dancing and singing beneath the peristyle. Devotion to the *houngan* and obedience are the main qualities required of the *hounsi*. The leading *hounsi* can become the mistress of the choir during ceremonies: she controls what is sung and how, she identifies the *loa*s as they appear, and she has an important a role as the *laplace*, or priest's assistant.

No account of the dignitaries of the *hounfors* can be complete without reference to music and drumming, which is the linchpin of the vaudou ceremony. There are theatrical aspects to the drumming and music in the vaudou ceremony. The drummers do not have to be initiated, but they must be masters of the various rhythms, because a talented drummer is capable of inducing possession but an unskilled one can throw the ceremony into confusion. Night after night they must beat their instruments at a frenzied pace. Along with a repertoire of vaudou songs, drummers must be able to manage the polyrhythms that are part of vaudou drumming. Such talent is the fruit of prolonged apprenticeship, and a good drummer can acquire a national reputation. Vaudou drums are never played individually but always in groups of three. They are the same shape but different in size. The large drum is called the *manman*, the middle one the *segond*, and the smallest one the *bula*. They are all held and beaten differently—some with sticks, some without. The orchestra is dominated by the *manman*, which has the power to make the *loa*s appear. Drums may vary from one ritual to another, but they are all considered sacred. Perhaps the most spectacular drum is the six-foot-high *assotor*: considered the most sacred of the drums, it disappeared with the antisuperstitious campaign of the 1940s.

The vaudou ceremony itself is hardly the orgiastic ritual that has been reported by thrill-seeking visitors to Haiti. The stereotype of barbaric practices is probably related to particular elements in the vaudou ceremony, the sacrifice and possession. Once the god has been invoked with his or her own ritualistic formula, a *veve*, or geometrical symbol, is traced on the ground of the peristyle. Through these drawings the spirits are summoned. The next phase is the sacrifice, which is seen as a way of both honoring the gods and making them more powerful. The vaudou sacrifice concentrates in an animal—a chicken, goat, or pig—certain sacred properties that are liberated in the animal's immolation. This is a highly ritualized but bloody procedure. The animals' blood is also usually drunk by participants because it is assumed to have supernatural powers. Sacrificial animals are not chosen at random; each group of deities has its preferences. For instance, a major problem was created in Haiti when the black Haitian pig sacred to the *loa*s was exterminated by USAID because of a swine fever epidemic. The replacement pigs, which had been flown in from the United States, could not be sacrificed because they were not considered fit offerings to the *loa*s.

The other dramatic feature of vaudou worship, possession, is not an ordinary seizure; the worshiper might wait years for the phenomenon to take place. When the individual is finally possessed, or mounted, by a *loa*, that deity is called his or her *mait tet* (master of the head) as a recognition of the devotee's subservience to this spirit. The explanation for the trance into which the vaudou practitioner falls is that the spirit enters an individual after first driving out the person's *gro bon ange*, or soul. The eviction of the soul results in the trembling and convulsions that precede the *loa*'s manifestation in the body of the devotee. From then on, the god's personality takes over, and the relationship between the spirit and the possessed is likened to that of a rider and his horse. The possessed are prevented from doing harm to themselves by the rest of the faithful. Contact with the spirit results in a kind of drunkenness in an individual, who can remain in a trancelike state for hours or even days. Once the initial frenzied convulsions are over, the priest escorts the possessed to the *baji*, where he or she is dressed or given the attributes of the *loa* who has been invoked. The individual has now become the god and can dispense favors, threaten sinners, and give advice. Strange exploits have been reported during this phase of possession, as the individual in whom the god has vested its powers acquires extraordinary abilities.

One of the common beliefs about Haiti is the prevalence of sorcery. The vaudou doll is a staple of sensationalist accounts of magic in Haiti. Because of the widespread belief in magic in the Haitian countryside, vaudou priests are frequently called on to provide healing baths, potions, and powders. However, there is a general tendency to make a distinction between vaudou and magic. Given the nature of religious practice in vaudou, the vast number of worshipers are more interested in petitioning the *loa*s than in manipulating them to do evil. The most common manifestation of magic in Haitian culture is fear of the evil eye, or *maldioc*. Charms, or *wanga*, are frequently worn to ward off the effect of the glance that can cause you harm. The *houngan* is also consulted if it is felt that an individual has made a bargain with the evil spirits, or *baka*. Similarly, the *zombie*, or state of suspended animation induced by a *bocor*, is felt to enslave some individuals for life. Whenever someone dies suddenly and the cause is unknown, evil is suspected. Quite often the corpse is mutilated, or a woman who died a virgin is deflowered, to prevent it from being used afterwards by an unscrupulous *bocor* for evil purposes. In an atmosphere of credulity and ignorance, the Haitian peasant needs explanations for things that appear mysterious or threatening. Consequently, many Haitians are persuaded that evil lurks behind the apparently normal. Despite the fact that the penal code explicitly forbids magic, quite often mobs summarily execute individuals thought to be practitioners of sorcery or capable of becoming *zobop* (werewolves).

Despite the lack of an institutional structure, a prevailing orthodoxy, or any kind of national organization, vaudou has come to be seen as a profound part of Haiti's religious culture, all the more alive because it is so elusive and mysterious. Vaudou has now been exported to areas of North America with large concentrations of Haitians. There is documented evidence of vaudou's ability to travel without having a formalized, written orthodoxy.[6] This is clear indication of the durability and the adaptability of this people's religion. Vaudou now has what amounts to a public relations organization called Zantray, which stands for Children of the Haitian Tradition and also means "innards" or "heart." The 1987 constitution reaffirmed the right of all Haitians to freely practice the religion of their choice. Generally, vaudou is now seen as less of a threat or a hindrance than it was in the past. President Aristide, in an unprecedented spirit of ecumenism, welcomed vaudou priests to the national palace at his inauguration in 1991.

NOTES

1. James Leyburn, *The Haitian People*, rev. ed. (New Haven, CT: Yale University Press, 1966), 129–130.

2. Wade Davis, *The Serpent and the Rainbow* (London: Collins, 1986), 171.

3. Leyburn, *The Haitian People*, 113.

4. Amy Wilentz, *The Rainy Season: Haiti Since Duvalier* (New York: Touchstone, 1989), 188.

5. Alfred Metraux, *Voodoo in Haiti* (London: Andre Deutsch, 1959), 56–57.

6. Karen McCarthy Brown, *Mama Lola: A Vodou Priestess in Brooklyn* (Berkeley: University of California Press, 1991).

4

Social Customs

IN AN ACCOUNT of the last forty years of Haitian art, the author speculates about an often-observed paradox in Haitian society. Given that Haiti is the poorest country in the Western Hemisphere, with many of its citizens close to starvation and with future prospects so uncertain, why is there so much joy in Haitian culture?

> What is the source of this joy? . . . Why in Haiti of all places? In even the most favored societies today, artists seem to be obsessed with war, poverty, injustice, brutish commercialism, and hedonism; or are so incapable of dealing guiltlessly with these themes that they try to psychoanalyze their incapacities or escape from them entirely.[1]

Whether we accept this explanation or not, we are certain to be struck by the tremendous amount of joie de vivre that is reflected in the behavior, attitudes, and self-expression of the poorest Haitian. This does not mean that we should succumb to enraptured elegies to the simple virtues of Haiti's happy poor. However, there has perhaps been too much of a tendency to accentuate the image of the *tristes tropiques* ("sad tropics") or indulge in the dark melancholy of a Graham Greene when he looks at Haiti under Duvalier. The look of the horrified traveler ignores the Haitian's relation to this world and the stubborn, resolute pleasure and creativity that is apparent whenever culture is performed or expressed. It is often through the changing performances in popular culture that a change in the collective consciousness of a people can be discerned. Haiti is no different in this regard. The vast majority of Haitians still live outside the cities. In rural Haiti, one is as much struck by the friendly nature of the average peasant as saddened by the harsh conditions of life.

ENTERTAINMENT

There is little in terms of entertainment and organized sports in Haiti. Nightlife in Port-au-Prince is limited to the lucky few who can get to the discotheques of Petionville or the floor shows at the various hotels. The Oloffson Hotel is particularly privilege since it is operated by the bandleader of Ram, Richard Morse, and the band regularly performs at this hotel in Port-au-Prince. Given the wealth of literary talent in Haiti, there should be more theatre. There was a time in the 1950s when the Theatre de Verdure on Harry Truman Boulevard on the waterfront was a popular venue for plays. The turbulent politics of the last four decades have taken their toll, and the only theatre that is available is sponsored by the Institut Francais. The French Institute, with its 350-seat auditorium, is the largest theatre in the country and has replaced the Rex cinema as a venue for drama. One of the country's best troupes is led by the distinguished actor Hervé Denis, who was once proposed as Haiti's prime minister but was never ratified by the very divided parliament. Denis has done some very successful adaptations of Aimé Cesaire's epic theatre. However, his audience is limited to the thousand or so members of the middle and upper class. His theatre is limited also because it is in French. However, even if the plays were in Creole, not many Haitians can afford the U.S. $4 to see a theatrical production. There is a more popular theatre that is largely slapstick comedy in Creole. Out of this form of escapist theatre, the popular comedian Languichatte emerged.

FOOD

Even though a significant portion of the Haitian population barely exists above the poverty line and depends on food from USAID in order to survive, there is a tradition of Creole cuisine in Haiti. One of the most popular poems of the Indigenous movement was Emile Roumer's "Marabout de mon Coeur" (Marabout of My Heart), which has been put to music and almost has the same status of songs like "Choucoune" (name of a female persona) and "Haiti Cherie" (Dear Haiti). The success of this work is related to the fact that it compares the woman to whom the poem is dedicated to a series of local dishes, including the best known of Haitian specialties, *riz djon djon*, or rice with black mushrooms. Other specialty dishes include *lambi*, a stew made from the meat of the conch; *griot*, which is fried pork; *tasot d'inde*, or dried turkey; *accras de morue*, or salt fish fritters, and *pain patate*, or sweet potato pudding. A favorite beverage is *acassan au sirop*, which is very thick and sweet. The best known soup is *soupe au giraumon* (pumpkin soup), which is served on Sundays and on January 1, the day on which Haitian independence is celebrated. If there is a national drink it is *clairin*, which is a homemade rum, often used in aromatic drinks called *trempés*.

POPULAR FESTIVITIES

In an attempt to dispel the impression that drums at night in rural Haiti means sinister goings-on under the cover of darkness, one author makes the observation that it is nothing more than a neighborhood dance with smutty songs, crude speech, and poking fun at famous people.[2]

The passion for music and dance is characteristic of popular entertainment in Haiti. Outside the normal Saturday *bamboche*, or party, the most remarkable of the forms of popular entertainment is the *ra ra* band, which is associated with the season of Lent and with Good Friday in particular. These Christian holidays are linked with vaudou, and the bands frequently come out at night. Easter is the highpoint of *ra ra* celebrations. On Easter Sunday *ra ra* bands flow from the vaudou temples through the streets of Haitian towns. Musicians blowing long bamboo tubes, or *vaccins*, accompany them. The rest of the music is usually made up of percussion instruments improvised from anything that can be knocked together. There can be a somewhat intimidating element in these bands: men may be costumed as women and the groups might be led by a figure wielding a whip. They tend to be feared by the middle class. Children especially are taught to see them as evil. The *angaje* (politically committed) musicians have appropriated the subversive image of the *ra ra* group in recent times in order to authenticate their songs of protest.

The *ra ra* bands can be seen as an offshoot of Carnival, the festivities held on the Sunday, Monday, and Tuesday preceding Ash Wednesday. Carnival is about costume, and in Haiti there are many traditional costumed figures that appear on the streets during Carnival time. Bats, various hideous masks, and pre-Columbian Indians are favored. Because Haitians do not have much money to spend on costumes, however, music assumes an enormous importance at Carnival time. The idea behind Carnival music is to fuse music, dance, and emotion. The kind of excitement and exuberance that is generated is called *enraje*, or "violently turned-on." At dramatic points in the music, when the crowd is really worked up, or *chofe*, both hands are raised in the air as the dancers are captivated by the rhythms and the refrain. The move-ment of paroxysm in Carnival is called *coudyay*, from the French *coup de jaille* or violent explosion. The floats and bands are provided by commercial enterprises. However, after the elite have enjoyed the theatrical spectacle, the streets belong to the masses. Carnival has traditionally been seen in Haiti as an outlet for the frustrations of the masses. The Duvaliers regularly used it to gain favor with the people. However, as the military regime that overthrew President Aristide also recognized, Carnival and its music can be a potent force for protest and directing the people's resentment.

There are other less formalized festivities that are traditionally performed, like the wakes for the dead, which are accompanied by storytelling, riddles, and religious songs. One much-favored pastime is betting on the lottery or *borlette*. Dreams have a great influence on numbers chosen for a bet. The weekly draw is made in the Dominican Republic on Sundays.

SPORTS

Despite inroads made by basketball because of cable television, soccer is the national passion, and matches at the Sylvio Cator Stadium in Port-au-Prince attract large crowds. Haiti shares Latin America's enthusiasm for the game, which generally can be seen as a unifying element of this very divided country. You are very likely to see improvised soccer matches throughout Haiti, because the possibility of a professional career in the game is a dream shared by many young men. The importance of World Cup matches is such that the business of government must take into consideration the schedule of matches, especially if Brazil's team is playing. Haiti's national team has never been important internationally. However, it invariably makes a good showing regionally, demonstrating that it is a force to be reckoned with in Caribbean competitions.

The most popular traditional national pastime is undoubtedly the cock fight; it is the sport of choice for the Haitian peasantry. The cocks all have names, and the sport is practiced at a local pit or *gaguere*. Betting is part of this activity. The spectators and owners assemble around the pit, and there is frequent comment on the fight as well as advice to the owner. Between rounds the cock is sprayed with rum, his spurs are filed sharp, and he is made excited to go back into the ring. The betting becomes more enthusiastic and the screams louder as the fight becomes more bloody. The object of the fight is to destroy the opponent's bird; a fight can last up to half an hour, de-pending on the viciousness of the birds. The final moments of any cockfight are not for the squeamish because of the gory nature of the combat.

The importance of this combat to the death, as well as the symbolism of the fighting cock, has not been lost on politicians. President Aristide's electoral symbol was the fighting cock; it is frequently painted on walls along with his picture. The fighting cock is a potent political symbol for the battle for a new Haiti that is being played out in national politics. It is as much a symbol of the fight to the death as it is the possible herald of a new dawn for a much embattled society.[3]

NOTES

1. Selden Rodman, *Where Art Is Joy* (New York: Ruggles de la Tour, 1988), 10.

2. James Leyburn, *The Haitian People* (New Haven CT: Yale University Press, 1966), 296.

3. Michele Wucker, *Why the Cocks Fight* (New York: Hillard Wang, 1999). This study of Dominican-Haitian relations uses the cockfight as a means of analyzing politics in the two rival republics.

Haiti's gleaming white National Palace.

François Duvalier presenting his son Jean Claude Duvalier.

Electoral poster showing candidates for president and how to vote.
Photo by J. Peter Costantini, 1995.

School children in Port-au-Prince wear uniforms.
Photo by J. Peter Costantini, 1995.

Boys stand on the wall of a fort overlooking the Artibonite valley in central Haiti.
Photo by J. Peter Costantini, 1995.

Brightly painted "tap-taps," small private buses, provide public transportation.

Boys play with irrigation machinery on the Estere River in central Haiti.
Photo by J. Peter Costantini, 1995.

Horses are the primary means of individual transportation for farmers in Ti Rivye.
Photo by J. Peter Costantini, 1995.

Farmer shows his harvest of millet in the Artibonite valley.
Photo by J. Peter Costantini, 1995.

Women in the Artibonite valley carry loads on their heads.
Photo by J. Peter Costantini, 1995.

Firewood sellers in Ti Rivye. Photo by J. Peter Costantini, 1995.

Fruit and vegetable vendor in Kenscoff. Photo by J. Peter Costantini, 1995.

Street market in Port-au-Prince in front of traditional houses.
Photo by J. Peter Costantini, 1995.

Market vendor cuts sugar cane in pieces to sell.
Photo by J. Peter Costantini, 1995.

Furniture maker weaves wicker. Photo by J. Peter Costantini, 1995.

Metalworkers display traditional Haitian enamelled metal plaques outside their Port-au-Prince shop. Photo by J. Peter Costantini, 1995.

Traditional houses in Ti Rivye. Photo by J. Peter Costantini, 1995.

Colonial building in Port-au-Prince serves as a government ministry.
Photo by J. Peter Costantini, 1995.

Former military barracks in Port-au-Prince. Haiti's military was abolished by President Jean-Bertrand Aristide and replaced by a civilian police force. Photo by J. Peter Costantini, 1995.

Town hall of Ti Rivye, Petite Riviere de l'Artibonite in French. Photo by J. Peter Costantini, 1995.

Jacques Roumain, Haiti's best-known novelist.

Jacques Stephen Alexis, a writer killed in 1961.

Hector Hippolyte, Vaudou Priest with one of his paintings.

Wilson Bigaud and one of his crowded canvases.

Untitled painting by Prospère Pierre Louis.

5

Mass Media and Cinema

ONE OF THE most visible features of downtown Port-au-Prince today is the spray-painted graffiti that is emblazoned on the walls of Haiti's decrepit capital city. Walls are covered with a haphazard patchwork of political graffiti, transforming the city into a Creole billboard of political slogans and social commentary. Churches, schools, and even cemeteries are used to disseminate the views of diverse political organizations that need the street to protest or campaign for various political figures. These heavily daubed walls can be seen as an expression of popular enthusiasm for the newfound liberties that have come to ordinary Haitians. They also point to the fact that in this impoverished country the majority of the population does not have television sets, radios, and telephones. This improvised method of political debate is probably also related to the fact that the high illiteracy rate makes newspapers a less than effective means of communication. Simplified messages painted in public spaces have become the preferred means of ventilating local issues in a country where there is 80 percent illiteracy and a wealthy minority has access to Ted Turner's Cable News Network on its satellite dishes.

It is, therefore, impossible to discuss the state of the mass media in Haiti without first taking into account the high levels of illiteracy in the population and the limited access to the electronic media in the poorest country in the Western Hemisphere. For the longest while, both poverty and illiteracy helped enormously in establishing authoritarian politics in Haiti. The inaccessibility of the media, especially in rural Haiti, and the inability to read meant that even if information were available, it could have little impact on the majority of the population. For instance, reports of human rights violations and of infringements of press freedom have generally been available to Haitians ever since the fall of Jean Claude Duvalier in 1986 and even during the coup that forced President Aristide into exile. However, the fact that these reports were in a printed form and, furthermore, written in French, which is the language of a small minority, meant that they were no threat to those in power. Indeed, this free circulation of information, which would be unthinkable in neighboring Cuba, for example, can actually enhance a repressive regime's image of tolerance of criticism and respect for the media.

PRINT MEDIA

In general, the newspapers printed in Haiti are tame and mediocre in quality, compared to the more outspoken and more partisan weeklies that are printed in New York and Miami. They are all sold on the roadside by vendors who take advantage of the traffic jams to target prospective customers. However, despite the fact that there seems to be a reasonably extensive choice, with half a dozen newspapers available at any given time, the circulation is predictably low. The most prominent and arguably the most bland Haitian newspaper, *Le Nouvelliste*, is more than 100 years old. It is, however, a thin and boring daily that has a print-run of 6,000 copies in a country whose population is estimated at more than seven million. This is the largest circulation for Haitian newspapers. However, it would not be in the paper's best interest to be more outspoken. In the past this could have led to repression and persecution by the authorities—for a more aggressive editorial policy that would have had no effect on the population, anyway, since it was written in French.

The journalistic pen has never been mightier than the sword in Haiti. From the very outset, there were conflicts between freedom of expression, which the press was tempted to exercise, and the dictatorial reflexes of the Haitian state. This was as true of the planters during the colonial period in their efforts to prevent the freedoms unleashed by the French Revolution from disrupting colonial St. Domingue as it was during the U.S. occupation or during the Duvalier regime. Newspapers have been as numerous as they have been ephemeral. Hundreds of newspapers have been published since independence in 1804. Of these, only *Le Nouvelliste*, founded in 1898, and *Le Matin*, launched in 1907, still exist. Their survival is closely related to their moderate nature and their adaptability to political circumstances.

As a rule the Haitian press has been influential only in political activity among members of the elite. Haitian literary history is filled with journals and magazines that have at one time or another been involved in fierce literary

and political debates. These papers have generally never outlasted the movement or the ideology that produced them. In the twentieth century, for
instance, protest of the U.S. occupation led to the creation of newspapers
such as *La Patrie* in 1915 and *L'Union Patriotique* in 1920 by the talented
poet Georges Sylvain, who ceased writing poetry in order to involve himself
fully in journalism. Student activists in the 1920s also turned to journalism
as a way of mobilizing the literate elite against the U.S. presence. Similarly,
the anti-superstitious campaign in the early 1940s produced a remarkable
debate in the press between Jacques Roumain criticizing the Catholic Church
in the pages of *Le Nouvelliste* in response to articles denigrating vaudou in
the Catholic newspaper *La Phalange*. Again the turbulent events of 1946
produced a flurry of ideological activity, which created a number of political
newspapers such as *La Ruche, La Nouvelle Ruche, Combat, La Presse* and
L'Action Nationale. Indeed, every important political event in Haiti since the
occupation has produced vigorous public debate in a number of ideologically
based newspapers. Journalism has always been seen as a worthy activity of
the traditional Haitian man of letters. A description of the mulatto liberal
Edouard Tardieu, who started the small newspaper *L'Action Sociale* in the
1940s, is amusingly accurate in depicting the high-mindedness of the mulatto
intellectual cum journalist and the absence of women from politics:

> Monsieur Edouard Tardieu was leader of the Christian Social Party in
> the election of 1946 and edited the party's newspaper, the columns of
> which were filled principally with reports of his speeches. On the back
> page, however, a regular feature was an advertisement for Madame
> Tardieu's grocery shop. While he was upstairs writing speeches, she was
> downstairs managing the family business making sure that their budget
> could support the political adventures of her husband. This is not en-
> tirely atypical of the situation among the elite in Haiti.[1]

This history of limited but vigorous partisan activity of the press was the
main reason it did not survive the repression of the Duvalier regime. It was
an early casualty of the Duvalier regime because it was seen as a potential
area of opposition from members of the elite. A number of presses were
destroyed in the 1960s, and even the Catholic newspaper *La Phalange* was
forced to close in 1961. Haitians depended on external sources like the Voice
of America and Radio Havana for reliable news. The situation remained
largely unchanged for the entire period of Francois Duvalier's presidency.
Between 1957 and 1971 censorship in Haiti was rigidly enforced, and no
local publisher or newspaper was allowed to print stories on local politics.

Some, like the editor of the daily *Le Nouveau Monde*, were driven to the absurd extreme of treating Duvalier as if he were a divine leader. Even foreign magazines and newspapers imported into Haiti were not spared, as state censors would regularly cut out articles they considered subversive or critical of Duvalier.

Political liberalization under Duvalier's son was also extended to the media. In his desire to improve his image abroad and to impress the Carter Administration with his tolerance of freedom of expression, Jean Claude Duvalier allowed journalists to be more outspoken. *Le Nouveau Monde*, the official voice of Duvalierism, continued its sycophantic tone, but new and bolder publications like *Le Petit Samedi Soir* emerged. This weekly, which began in 1975, not only became very popular but its editor, Dieudonné Fardin, found a way of being both ingratiating and critical at the same time. Fardin's politics were viewed with ambivalence by many, but his weekly did pioneer dissent with the regime. In 1977 the first paper to denounce the brutalities of the regime and question presidency for life was *Hebdo Jeune Presse*. It did not last long after the editor's father was beaten unconscious by Duvalier's Macoutes.

Alarmed that the press was becoming too vocal, Duvalier formed his own press agency to promote the virtues of *Jeanclaudisme*. However, the gains made in press freedom proved irreversible, especially under pressure from President Carter's special envoy to Haiti, Andrew Young. By 1980, a reluctant regime found itself facing an increasingly bold media and, for the first time, strikes and minor demonstrations. This liberal period coincided with Duvalier's extravagant wedding to Michele Bennett. The images of a rapacious elite and of misrule that led to widespread misery were widely disseminated both inside and outside Haiti and tarnished irrevocably Duvalier's reputation for liberal policies after this event. These gestures toward democratization were brought to an abrupt halt in November 1980 with the election of President Reagan and a change of U.S. policy on human rights. However, it was already too late to muzzle the media, which had had a taste of its power. Strict application was ordered of a 1979 law that prescribed harsh penalties for offensive references in the media to the president, his wife, and senior officials. Journalists were arrested and many deported, but the regime had been exposed as intolerant of dissent and capable of brutality behind its liberal facade. As the stories of Haitian boat people as well as reports of the shopping trips of the president wife made their way into the press, the end of the regime was becoming more apparent.

The countdown to the end of Jean Claude Duvalier's regime began in 1984 with staged elections and a new promise of democratization in an effort by the regime to meet the U.S. Congress's human rights performance certification, without which no further financial aid would be forthcoming. The ensuing political protests led to a desperate crackdown on the local media. Near the end of the Duvalier regime, a state of siege was declared and all independent presses silenced. The only newspaper worth reading at the time was the weekly *Le Petit Samedi Soir*, and even Fardin did not dare to cover sensitive political issues. The other supposedly independent dailies, such as *Le Nouvelliste* and *Le Matin*, reported on local political events by simply reproducing the brief dispatches from the Agence France Press representative.

It is during this period that Haitian newspapers published in the exile communities in New York and Miami came into their own. The latest scandals and excesses of the Duvalier regime were fully reported in the three main weeklies that originated in North America. *Haiti Observateur* is perhaps the biggest and best organized of the three major exile tabloids. It was founded by Raymond and Leo Joseph and is based in Brooklyn. Its politics are generally centrist, with a strong anti-Aristide line in recent times. This paper began publishing in 1971, the year that Jean Claude Duvalier came to power. It is written in French, English, and Creole and quite often has very good coverage of local news because of useful inside sources. It tends to contain more analysis of and commentary on the news than actual information. It contributed greatly to the fall of Jean Claude Duvalier and has had an effect on U.S. policy because of its bold and informed reporting as well as its strategic location in New York. It was not easily available in Haiti until the fall of the Duvalier in 1986. Its reading public still remains largely outside of Haiti, and consequently about a third of its coverage is devoted to the diaspora.

The two other newspapers edited in the United States are relatively leftist in orientation. *Haiti-Progres*, founded in 1983, is a New York–based weekly that emphasizes news coming from the provinces in Haiti and the working class. It also has pages in Creole and covers news from the Third World as a whole, especially South American countries. In Miami *Haiti en Marche* is published weekly by journalists who were originally expelled by Jean Claude Duvalier in 1980. Generally pro-Aristide, it specializes in political analysis of current events in Haiti. Since 1986, these newspapers have become very popular in Haiti and captured much of the local readership from the bland local publications. They have eclipsed the popularity of *Le Petit Samedi Soir*, which is now being criticized for having been too tame in the past. They are also understandably more appreciated than the older dailies, which only started showing some signs of life after having been overly docile in the past; it is difficult for them to shed their generally dull image. Even desperate attempts at renaming—such as with the Duvalierist *Le Nouveau Monde*, which was called *Haiti Libérée* after 1986 and then *L'Union*—cannot bring new life to publications that did very little to end Duvalierism in Haiti.

The cultural and linguistic aspect of *Haiti Observateur*, rather than its political orientation, points to important future developments in the Haitian media. It has a circulation of 75,000 copies weekly, of which two thirds are sold in the diaspora, and it is published in the three languages that will be important to Haiti's future: French, English, and Creole. It also usefully combines its political coverage, which often includes articles reproduced from major American newspapers, with reviews of Haitian music and the theatre. It also fosters an awareness of the links between the local Haitian community and the wider diaspora, which is a crucial aspect of contemporary Haitian identity. *Haiti Observateur* suffers, however, from a problem that afflicts all Haitian newspapers, the lack of trained journalists. The average Haitian journalist is in his or her twenties and learns on the job. What these people lack in training, they make up for in enthusiasm and an understanding of local issues. It is this untrained talent that makes for lively journalism in today's Haiti, whether in a multinational operation like *Haiti Observateur* or in the successful pro-Aristide weekly paper, *Libete*, which is written entirely in Creole.

ELECTRONIC MEDIA

The low rate of literacy in Haiti has meant that radio, not the newspapers, is the major source of news and entertainment for the majority of the Haitian population. Radio's beginnings date back to the 1920s and the U.S. occupation. At this time, broadcasting was dominated by elite tastes and the politics of the pliant, pro-American then-president, Louis Borno. However, the lack of radio sets in the country and limited programming made radio broadcasts relatively unimportant to Haitian life until well after the occupation. By the 1950s Radio d'Haiti, run by the Widmaier family, influenced musical tastes in Haiti because of increased hours of programming and improved technology. Radio came into its own in the last three decades with the advent of the cheap transistor radio and cassette player. Widespread availability of these sets, often brought back by returning Haitians from the United States, has meant that even poor Haitians, who have no electricity, are now relatively better informed than were previous generations. Radio was a vital part of the downfall of Duvalierism and today is an essential tool in disseminating political broadcasts and electoral information.

The importance of radio first became manifest in the feeble efforts at liberalization by Jean Claude Duvalier. In the late 1970s the regime set up Radio Nationale d'Haiti and Television Nationale d'Haiti in an effort to strengthen its propagandist thrust. However, it could not compete with the privately owned Radio Haiti Inter, whose journalists—in particular the late Jean Dominique and Compere Filo—had developed a popular local following. This station not only developed credibility with reports in Creole, it also gave ordinary Haitians the opportunity to complain on the air about mistreatment and injustice. Duvalier shut down the radio in 1980. The outspoken director, Jean Dominique, and the most popular journalists were sent into exile. A massive crowd at the airport greeted them in 1986 when they returned from exile. During the turbulent years before the election of 1990, the radio was often the target of military harassment, and its transmitter was destroyed in 1989 by the army.

With the press silenced and Radio Haiti Inter off the air, the religious stations in Haiti became centers for anti-Duvalierist mobilization. They were the only institutions with any hope of immunity from state interference, and they had already become very active in the countryside with literacy campaigns in Creole. The Catholic radio station Radio Soleil led the way. Supervised by foreign priests with a network of local journalists, Radio Soleil was created in 1978 in order to evangelize and improve literacy. It soon became the voice of the Ti Legliz, which represented Haiti's disenfranchised. The power of this station was first demonstrated in 1985 when it led a successful boycott of a referendum to endorse Duvalier's life-presidency. The Belgian director of the station was expelled, but its violent anti-Duvalier sermons remained in circulation on cassettes. The power of church congregations prevented the station from being completely shut down. The highpoint in the Church's activism came later in 1985, when troops shot dead four schoolchildren in Gonaives. If any attempt had been made to close the station, protests would automatically have ensued. Even when forbidden to broadcast news, Radio Soleil would have transmitted protest songs and sermons by politically activist priests like Father Aristide or Monsigneur Willy Romelus of Jérémie. The Catholic hierarchy attempted to change the activist orientation of the station in 1989 by changing the director, and the station has consequently not been very active in pressing for radical changes in Haiti.

The other important radio station is Radio Lumière. Like Radio Soleil, it was supervised by foreign priests, this time from the Baptist Church. Also like Radio Soleil, its broadcasts could be relayed to the entire country through Baptist missions situated all over mountainous Haiti. They contributed enormously to empowering the majority of Haitians by shifting their attention from the capital to the rural area and by placing reporters who could provide live eyewitness accounts of events as they took place. Radio Lumière was attacked in 1991 after it reported the army-led killing of Aristide's supporters in the slums; its studio and transmitter were destroyed. When one of its former directors was gunned down by the army, Radio Lumière limited itself to shorter broadcasts with no comment on local issues.

After 1986 there was a proliferation of radio stations, all of which took advantage of the unprecedented freedom of speech sweeping Haiti. Television stations have never been important to the majority of Haitians, even since 1986. Télé Haiti is a private station that requires an expensive subscription, and state television, Télévision Nationale d'Haiti, is tainted by its Duvalierist origins. One of the most innovative moves by a radio station in Haiti after Duvalierism was the creation of a talk show entitled *Libre Tribune* by Radio Antilles Internationale after Duvalier's departure. However, this show allowed Haitians to sound off on any topic they chose, so it soon created problems, as the army saw this exercise of press freedom as a threat. The eccentric journalist and former Duvalierist Serge Beaulieu, who is owner and director of Radio Liberté, tried a similar format. This station is all talk and allows listeners to phone in during an eight-hour evening show. Beaulieu manages to insult or annoy all sectors of the society on his station. If he continues to exist it is because his demagogic tirades have created an audience. Other stations of note are Tropic FM, which was frequently attacked by the Haitian army during the year of the coup that overthrew President Aristide. Its format was not commentary or analysis but brief items of news every half hour, which the de facto government of Raoul Cedras found difficult to tolerate. Another significant but more middle-class station is Radio Métropole, run by Richard Widmaier. It has been less daring in its news coverage but is respected because of the professionalism of its journalists.

The importance of radio stations to democratic freedoms in Haiti can be gauged by the silencing of all antigovernment media during the three years of the coup that ousted President Aristide. During this time the Haitian military set out to systematically dismantle the radio stations that had become so vital to communication and democratization in contemporary Haiti. The de facto regime required that all journalists be accredited through the Ministry of Information. Without this accreditation they would not be allowed to exercise their profession. A directive was also issued requiring all radio stations to abstain from broadcasting information liable to incite disorder. All news reports had to submitted to the government before being broadcast. These measures, as well as armed attacks on journalists and radio stations, effectively silenced the radio stations in Haiti. A way around the military's rigid censorship was found in the Catholic station Radio Enriquillo, which broadcast from the border of the Dominican Republic. This station became the only reliable source of uncensored news for Haitians. Besides offering detailed coverage of human rights abuses, Radio Enriquillo also featured interviews with Aristide and his supporters. The military government in Haiti complained to the Dominican Republic about the station's operation, and Radio Enriquillo was ordered to stop all news broadcasts in Creole. However, the station found an ingenious way to get around the government's order. News programs were set to music and station employees sung the news bulletins and press releases. Five months later, this too was declared illegal.

In the same way that Haitian newspapers established in North America have played an important role in linking local Haitian communities with those in the diaspora, Haitian radio stations in the United States have also been instrumental in keeping Haitians abroad informed about happenings at home. Stations in Washington, DC, Miami, Boston, and New York form important relays of information for Haitians on the outside. A number of small pirate Creole radio stations have also emerged in Haitian enclaves in the United States with names like Radio Lakay, Radio Etincelle, and Radio Galaxy. They often serve as the glue that holds Haitian communities together. These stations often share programming, and Radio Soleil d'Haiti, based in Brooklyn, broadcasts material from correspondents located in Haiti. They can also provide important links with non-Haitian media by providing commentaries and news for French, U.S., and Canadian radio programs. As with the newspaper reporters, many radio journalists worked at one time or another in Haiti. Many broadcast in French, Creole, and English in an effort to cover as wide as possible a cross-section of the Haitian diaspora. Often the language of some presenters is a creative and spontaneous combination of all three languages. Their base is essentially the Haitian community and they specialize in news from Haiti. They also do interviews with Haitian and American politicians who are seeking the political or financial support of the Haitian diaspora.

Radio is the preferred medium of public involvement in the country's affairs in Haiti. Audiocassettes, however, are the chief means of correspondence between Haitians. It has been noted that

> Illiteracy makes writing letters impossible for all but a small part of the population. Other Haitians communicate with their émigré relatives . . . by sending cassettes back and forth, and, as a result, Walkmans are more common than typewriters here, and often the first thing a new emigrant sends home is a tape recorder with a few cassettes.[2]

With the silencing of the radio stations, cassettes began to be used as a news medium. Gotson Pierre, who once worked with Radio Soleil, came up with a project to record news on cassettes for subscribers in 1989. The cassettes were thirty minutes long. They could be recorded by a group of journalists and then played back in private, completely undetected by the police. These cassettes of news, music, and commentary in Creole were made by groups of journalists, copied on high-speed machines, and distributed to subscribers in Haiti and in exile communities. Distribution in rural Haiti was done by different community organizations, and people sometimes pooled their resources to buy a cassette player.

CINEMA

Haitian cinema is not very well developed, and the number of films made in Haiti by Haitians can be counted on the fingers of one hand. Indeed, French Caribbean cinema as a whole is still in its infancy, and cinematographers are still few and far between. It has been observed that

> The Caribbean had a long acquaintance with cinema, but only as a resource for foreign productions which exploit(ed) the natural/physical endowment of the tropical islands and invented other endowments to manufacture an image of the Caribbean radically at odds with the reality of the people of the Caribbean.[3]

Not only is this true for the Caribbean, it is particularly damaging in the case of Haiti, as sensationalist images have always marked the depiction of the first black republic in the imagination of Hollywood. There has been some change in recent times as Caribbean filmmakers have begun to express a more credible picture of local realities. One of the best-known French Caribbean directors is Euzhan Palcy of Martinique. Her 1983 film, *La rue Cases-Negres* (Black Shack Alley), adapted from the Martiniquan novel by the same name, was both a popular and critical success. She went on to direct a big budget Hollywood version of *A Dry White Season* starring Marlon Brando. Change can also be seen in the relationship between literature and film as more French-speaking Caribbean writers become interested in the cinema. In Martinique, the novelist Patrick Chamoiseau has written the screenplay for *L'Exil de Behanzin* (1995), and the Haitian writer Dany Laferriere pinned the screenplay for his own novel, *How to Make Love with a Negro without Getting Tired*, which was released in Canada in 1990. Jean

Claude Charles has written the screenplay for a movie to be set in Berlin and directed by Raoul Peck.

In contrast to the impoverished state of Haitian cinema, foreign cinema-tographers have taken great interest in Haiti, its history and culture. In this area, the documentary rather than the feature film predominates. Documentary films about Haiti have their origin in the U.S. occupation, when the United States resorted to film as a way of spreading propagandist messages to the population. However, it was not until after the occupation that cinema really caught on in Haiti. Haiti's main cinema, the Rex in Port-au-Prince, was not constructed until 1935. There are reports that a Russian director, Sergei Eisenstein, had planned to make a film of the life of Henri Christophe, called *Black Majesty* and starring Paul Robeson, in the 1930s. This project never got off the ground.

One of the earliest and most successful documentary films made in Haiti was Maya Deren's *Divine Horsemen: The Living Gods of Haiti* in 1951. This documentary was originally part of an anthropological project to present the dances of the vaudou religion. The filmmaker became personally attracted to vaudou and made a film that is less documentary than homage to Haiti's glorious primitivism. The dramatic nature of Haitian social reality also at-tracted documentary filmmakers—for example, Haitian cane cutters (*Bitter Sugar*), boat people (*Voyage of Dreams*), Haitian workers in the Dominican Republic (*Via Crucis*), and the ironically entitled *Haiti, Perle des Antilles* dealing with the economic disparities in Haitian society. More recently, a well-known American director, Jonathan Demme, made a documentary on repression after the fall of the Duvaliers entitled *Haiti: Dreams of Democracy*. Although this is not the only attempt to film recent political events in Haiti, it is a fine example of this kind of filmmaking, and it cleverly uses Haitian popular music to tell the story of resistance to the Haitian army.

Feature films made about Haiti have generally been sensationalist, delib-erately exploiting images of unenlightened savagery for the North American market. The first major film to do so was *White Zombie* in 1932, which was inspired by William Seabrook's lurid travel book, *The Magic Island*. This film, which deals with the zombification of a white female visitor to Haiti, launched the stereotype of the zombie and black magic in the American imagination. These images were still very powerful in the film *The Serpent and the Rainbow*, made in 1988 by Wes Craven, the director of the horror movie *Nightmare on Elm Street*. In 1967 the film of Graham Greene's novel *The Comedians* was released; it was shot in Dahomey and starred Richard Burton and Elizabeth Taylor. This film was banned by the Duvalier govern-ment, which sued the director. Despite the genuine horrors of Duvalierism, the film does exploit the usual images of gratuitous savagery that are associated with Haiti. Less well known and far more accurate are the foreign films that use Haitian material for their scenarios. These are few, and the best known are the films made of Jacques Roumain's novel *Gouverneurs de la rosée*. In 1964 the film *Coumbite* was made by the Cuban director Tomas Guttierez, using Roumain's novel as its scenario. In 1974 Maurice Failvic shot *Gouverneurs de la rosée* for French television. This film, which used well-known Haitian actors, was a critical success in Haiti and in France, where it won the 1976 Critics' Award.

In recent times Haitians have made documentaries that are very political and are aimed at exposing the horrors of Duvalierism. Typical examples of this kind of filmmaking by Haitians are Ben Dupuy's *Haiti Enchaînée* (Haiti in Chains), Arnold Antonin's *Le Chemin de la Liberté* (Haiti: The Road to Freedom), and Antonin's *Les Duvaliers Condamnés* (The Duvaliers Indicted), all of which were shot in the mid-1970s. Antonin also did a short film in color entitled *Art Naif et Repression en Haiti* (Primitive Art and Repression in Haiti) and *Un Tonton Macoute Peut-il Devenir Poète?* (Can a Tonton Macoute Become a Poet?), both in 1975. Later Lucien Bonnet made *Ou Vas-Tu Haiti?* (Whither Haiti). By far the best-known Haitian documentary filmmaker is Elsie Haas, who lives in Paris. She has not concentrated on Haitian subjects in her work, choosing at times to document the lives of French West Indians in France. She has, however, done two remarkable documentaries on her homeland, *La Ronde des Tap Tap* (1986) and *La Ronde des Vodu* (1987). Both films were shot in Haiti immediately after the fall of the Duvalier regime. The first examines urban society in Haiti through the converted minivans and pickups that are called "Tap Taps" and used for public transportation. The second is her best film to date and explores the place of vaudou in contemporary Haiti. It surpasses Maya Deren's earlier film because it is not infatuated with peasant religion but puts it in a social and political context.

For feature films, there are only two filmmakers worthy of mention: Rassoul Labuchin (Yves Medard) and Raoul Peck. Labuchin, who is known as a poet, critic, and novelist, wrote the script in 1976 for a short Creole language film, *Map Pale Net* (I Speak Firmly), directed by Raphael Stines. It deals with the problems of a Haitian couple from the middle class and carefully avoids direct social commentary because of the Duvalier regime's sensitivity to criticism. Labuchin's second film project, *Anita*, was more ambitious and got him into trouble with Jean Claude Duvalier's regime. It was shot in the rural town of Miragoane and shown in 1980. It was quickly withdrawn from commercial circulation because of the crackdown on freedom of expression in the same year. This film, which is critical of social and economic realities but freely mixes reality and fantasy, is inspired by the novelist Jacques Stephen Alexis' concept of marvelous realism. *Anita* deals with the exploitative practice of child labor in Haiti. This image of servitude is used as a metaphor for the effect of U.S. imperialism on Haiti as well as for the cruelty of Haitians who take advantage of the less fortunate in that society. The two female protagonists in the film, Anita and Choupette, are both zombified by Haiti's social system. The film ends with solidarity between these two girls and an idealistic gesture of rebellion. This film was not meant as entertainment but to affect the conscience of a Haitian audience. Labuchin succeeded beyond his expectations: he was forced to seek exile in Mexico, where he spent a year, and, after a brief return to Haiti during which he was imprisoned, he was exiled to France.

Raoul Peck is the most critically acclaimed Haitian filmmaker to date because of his feature film *Haitian Corner*. Even his fellow director Rassoul Labuchin has conceded that it is the best film made by a Haitian. Peck's success is related to the fact that he operates outside Haiti, because the infrastructure for production, filming, and distribution in Haiti is almost nonexistent. He was also trained at the film academy in Berlin and is, like Elsie Haas, a professional filmmaker. *Haitian Corner* was shot in Brooklyn and stars, among others, the singer Toto Bissainthe. It derives its title from a Haitian bookshop bearing the same name. The story deals with an exiled Haitian, Joseph Bossuet, who is a factory worker and hangs out at this bookshop. He had been tortured by the Duvalier regime before choosing exile in New York. Unlike his fellow exiles, he cannot come to terms with his past, which haunts him in a series of nightmarish flashbacks. He happens to recognize one day one of the Macoutes who tortured him; he tracks him down and confronts him. His former torturer is now pleading for mercy as the situation between the two men is reversed. Bossuet, however, refuses to yield to revenge and lets his torturer go, thereby liberating himself from his disturbing past.

Peck's brilliant depiction of the individual's triumph over revenge is a promising commentary on the present state of Haitian society, which is itself attempting to place the Duvalierist nightmare in the past and move on to a more just and democratic society. Raoul Peck himself embodies the new Haitian identity that links the diaspora with the nation. He continues to produce films of high quality as can be seen in two recent documentaries, *Desounen* (Dialogue with Death) about the Haitian boat people, and an account of the career of the first prime minister of the Congo, Patrice Lumumba. His 1995 feature film *L'Homme sur le quai* (Man by the Shore), which deals with life in Haiti under Papa Doc as seen through the eyes of an abandoned 8-year-old girl, received much critical acclaim. After a short-lived and controversial term as minister of culture in Haiti, he now lives mostly abroad. If there are more directors like Raoul Peck and Elsie Haas, Haitian cinema may well have a place among the films that continue to flood Haiti from North America and Europe. The availability of films on video may well allow Haitians to eventually have access to their own material instead of having to rely exclusively on a commercial system of distribution.

NOTES

1. David Nicholls, *Haiti in Caribbean Context* (London: Macmillan, 1985), 121.

2. Anna Hurarska, "The First Casualty," *New Yorker*, April 19, 1993, 62.

3. Mbye Cham, *Ex-Iles: Essays on Caribbean Cinema* (Trenton, NJ: Africa World Press, 1992), 2.

6

Literature and Language

THE CULTURAL cleavage that has marked Haitian society politically and economically is also, not surprisingly, acutely apparent in the area of literary culture. The reasons for this kind of division between an elite, literary culture and a popular, oral one have as much to do with Haiti's French past as with the historical evolution of Haitian society. As we have seen, Haiti's history facilitated the emergence of two cultures, one urban and elite and the other rural and peasant. This means that the mass of Haiti's population could neither read nor could they afford to buy books. Haitian literature emerged from the declaration of independence in 1804, therefore, with a very restricted local reading public. However, despite this massive impoverished, nonreading public, those who wrote in Haiti have published more books than any other Caribbean country. The Haitian National Library estimates that since independence from France, Haitians have published about 17,000 titles. The vast majority of these have been in French, a language that 85 percent of the population is incapable of reading.

This urge among the Haitian elite to publish literary works is closely related to values assimilated from French colonialism. The French conception of culture and, consequently, French cultural policy have always placed a heavy emphasis on the universal, elite nature of a literary and intellectual culture and correspondingly despised those nonliterate cultures that did not fit into this universal idea. This attitude created in Haiti, as in other French Caribbean colonies, an enormous divide between French and Creole cultures and never allowed for a cultural continuum that would have spawned a range of intermediate forms of cultural and linguistic expression as existed in the anglophone Caribbean countries, for example. Such cultural influences have combined with the acute divisions in Haitian society to produce a remarkable disparity between a hyperliterate elite and a peasantry cut off from the mainstream of a French-oriented universal culture.

The elite's persistence in pursuing a literary culture is also particularly striking given the chaotic nature of Haitian politics. The ideal of free expression has never really been tolerated by the vast majority of political regimes in Haiti, and writers have often found themselves persecuted by the state, which invariably has seen their ideas as a threat to its existence. The most infamous of the Haitian regimes that persecuted writers and intellectuals was that of Francois Duvalier (1957–1971). During Papa Doc's rule, and to a lesser extent under Jean Claude Duvalier, books were banned, magazines were not allowed to print stories about local politics, and book publishing was stifled. Because of the assiduousness of state censors, it has been reported that entire rooms in the main post office in Port au Prince were stacked to the ceiling with books confiscated from the mail. The persecution of Haitian writers was a persistent feature of Duvalier's dictatorship in the late 1960s and reached a macabre level in 1971 with the murder by the Tonton Macoutes of a well-known Haitian novelist, Jacques Stephen Alexis.

EARLY NATIONALIST WRITING

The declaration of Haitian independence, drafted by Boisrond Tonnerre in 1804, is widely held to be the first example of writing coming from Haiti. Much of the nationalist literature in the nineteenth century takes its cue from this document. Pride in the historic defeat of Napoleon's army, the need to inspire the ideal of nationhood in the fledging state, and the desire to proclaim Haiti's redemptive mission in a world still dominated by slavery permeate the writing of Haitians in early post-independence years. Despite the instability of these early years, there is evidence of intense literary activity among the urban elite. The emergence of literary journals like *L'Abeille Haytienne* (The Haitian Bee, 1817) and Herard Dumesle's *L'Observateur* (The Observer, 1819) are clear signs of literary activity. The fierce literary nationalism of this period is strongly influenced by French Romanticism. Such themes as the quest for national identity, the importance of the individual imagination, the need to document Haitian culture and history in all its details, and the influence of landscape over the imagination are prevalent at this time. During the twenty-three years of relative stability under President Boyer, a literary elite established itself, and the first calls for a national literature were made in the pages of a newspaper called *Le Républicain* (The

Republican), founded by Ignace and Emile Nau along with the Ardouin brothers. The writers associated with this early expression of Haitian Indigenism argued strongly against imitativeness in Haitian literature, especially the use of classical forms and references in the poetry of the time. They felt that literature was important to earning the respect of a largely hostile world and that there was a real possibility of producing original literature from Haiti's unique, hybrid Afro-Latin heritage in the New World.

This desire to create a distinctive national literature was the point of departure for the success of the two major poets of what is known as the patriotic school in nineteenth century in Haiti—Oswald Durand and Massillon Coicou. Oswald Durand (1840–1906), heavily influenced in his early verse by the French Romantic poets Victor Hugo and Leconte de Lisle, went on to create in his major work, *Rires et Pleurs* (Laughter and Tears, 1896), a veritable inventory of Haitian landscape and culture. This deeply nationalistic verse was often used to rally Haitians to the ideals of national independence at a time when Haiti was politically threatened from both inside and outside. He is most often remembered for his poem about unrequited love, "Choucoune," which was written in Creole. This is the only case in Haitian literature where a literary work became a well-known folksong, as "Choucoune" was put to music in 1883 by a pianist from New Orleans, Michel Mauleart Monton. Durand's contemporary, Massillon Coicou (1867–1908) was both a poet and a dramatist. He was executed for conspiring against the government in 1908 and may be the first major writer from Haiti to have been executed by the state. He is best known for his tellingly named *Poésies nationales* (National poetry, 1892), which concentrates on the retelling of Haitian history and the struggle for independence.

No survey of writing in nineteenth-century Haiti could be complete without reference to Haiti's pamphleteers and essayists, who were at least as important as the creative writers. The first of these was Le baron de Vastey, the secretary of Haiti's short-lived king, Henri Christophe. His remarkable critique of colonialism, *Le système colonial dévoilé* (The colonial system unveiled, 1914), was the first Caribbean essay criticizing colonialism and arguing for decolonization. This tradition of the polemical essay continued into the late nineteenth century with a number of vigorous defenses of Haiti against theories of racial inferiority current in Europe at the time. For instance, in response to Gobineau's *Essai sur l'inégalité des races humaines* (Essay on the inequality of the human races), which argued that the black race was incapable of civilization, three major polemical works were produced. The titles of these publications speak for themselves: Louis Joseph Janvier's *L'égalité des races* (The equality of the races, 1884), Antenor Firmin's *De l'égalité des races humaines* (Concerning the equality of the races, 1885) and Hannibal Price's *De la réhabilitation de la race noire* (Concerning the rehabilitation of the black race, 1900).

The prose form that dominates the nineteenth century is the essay. The novel does not make its appearance until 1859 with the publication of *Stella* by Emeric Bergeaud. In the first decade or so of the twentieth century, Haiti's novelists made up for lost time by producing more than a dozen titles. These works are predictably marked by concern with Haiti's social and political problems. To this extent, these novels are closely related to the polemical essays mentioned earlier in that fiction becomes a vehicle for airing national issues, and characters are quite often simply mouthpieces for the author. The best known of these early novelists is Frédéric Marcelin (1848–1917), who founded the journal *Haiti Littéraire et Sociale* (Literary and Social Haiti) in 1905 and wrote three novels, of which the most accomplished is the political satire *Thémistocle-Epaminondas Labasterre* (1901). Other novels of note are Justin Lherisson's *La famille des Pitite-Caille* (The Pitite-Caille family, 1905), Antoine Innocent's *Mimola* (1906), and Fernand Hibbert's *Le manuscrit de mon ami* (My friend's manuscript, 1910). While being blatantly polemical in intent, these novels contained a level of documentary realism and specific cultural and linguistic references that paved the way for many important novels in the Indigenous tradition later in the century.

It is precisely this sometimes excessive concern with local color that produced a backlash at the beginning of the twentieth century from those writers who believed that Haitian literature was likely to fall into the trap of a merely local exoticism and, therefore, lose both the respect of the international community and the ability to produce works of major quality. Reaction against what what was seen as the parochialism of these early novelists came from a group of poets associated with the literary journal *La Ronde* (1898–1902). They argued for eclecticism in Haitian literature rather than a narrow regionalism. The work of the major poets of this period—Etzer Vilaire, Georges Sylvain, and Edmond Laforest—is marked by the impersonal, allusive aesthetic of the Symbolist movement in France. The poetry of Etzer Vilaire received the recognition of the Académie Française, and as a whole the writing of this group was as distinct from that of the novelists of the time as it was from the patriotic verse of its predecessors. This debate on the future of a national literature for Haiti was abruptly cut short by the U.S. occupation in 1915, which marked the beginning of modern Haitian writing.

POST-OCCUPATION WRITING

The nineteen years of the U.S. occupation united Haiti in a way that no Haitian president ever managed to do. Notoriously divided by class and color when left on their own, Haitians were united in the name of nation and race in the face of the white neocolonial presence of the U.S. Marines. Literary activity now acquired a new urgency. For instance, Georges Sylvain turned away from the literary abstractions of *La Ronde* and founded *L'Union Patriotique* to protest U.S. atrocities during the occupation. Another poet, Edmond Laforest, committed suicide by drowning when he learned of the intervention in 1915. These actions symbolized the end of a traditional conception of literary activity and the man of letters and the emergence a younger, more radical generation of Haitian writers who began to dominate Haitian literature in the 1920s.

This generation launched modern Haitian literature with the movement they called *indigenisme*. This movement was marked by the cultural politics of the time. It was driven by a fierce nationalism and anti-U.S. Sentiment and was equally critical of what was seen as the elitism of earlier generations of writers. The iconoclasm and anti-establishment attitudes of this movement became apparent in the pages of such journals as *La Nouvelle Ronde* (The New Round, 1925), *La Trouée* (The Breach, 1927), and, most importantly, *La Revue Indigène* (The Indigenous Review, 1927–1928). The ideas current at this time were influenced by the nationalism of the French political journalist Charles Maurras. His authoritarian politics influenced the thinking of key members of this generation. It was also felt that Haiti's intellectual and cultural isolation should come to an end. A conscious effort was therefore made to introduce Haitian writers to the literature of South American writers and of the Harlem Renaissance.

The main writers of this literary renaissance were Emile Roumer, Jacques Roumain, Carl Brouard, and Philippe Thoby-Marcelin. Emile Roumer (1903–1988) produced the first work to be considered identifiably "indigeniste." His *Poèmes d'Haiti et de France* (Poems of Haiti and France) appeared in 1925 and were published even before he became a founding member of *La Revue Indigène* in 1927. This would be his most important contribution to Haitian letters. Technically accomplished but conservative in style, he played no important part in subsequent movements; later in his life he became an ardent defender of the literary value of Creole. Philippe Thoby-Marcelin was an important contemporary of Roumer. After founding the ephemeral literary magazine *La Nouvelle Ronde*, he became one of the chief collaborators in *La Revue Indigène*, in which he published delicate mood poems inspired by Haitian peasant themes. He later achieved recognition with the sometimes humorous peasant novels he published with his younger brother Pierre: *Canape vert* (1942), *La bête de musseau* (The Beast of the Haitian hills, 1946), *Le crayon de dieu* (The pencil of God, 1952), and *Tous les hommes sont fous* (All men are mad, 1970).

Carl Brouard (1902–1965) was the most notoriously bohemian and mystical of the poets of Haitian *indigenisme*. Carl Brouard was the son of a wealthy Lebanese businessman and onetime mayor of Port-au-Prince, Raphael Brouard. Carl established his reputation as a poet very early with verse published in *La Revue Indigène*. From the outset, very much in the tradition of the French *poéte maudit*, he was obsessed with life in the slums of Port au Prince and the vaudou religion. The influence of the nineteenth-century French poet Charles Baudelaire is evident in his evocation of alcohol, debauchery, and sensual escapism in his indigenist poems. Less explicitly political than many of his contemporaries, Brouard concentrated on peasant religion as a way of going beyond local color to achieve an intense level of cultural authenticity. He also celebrated Haiti's African past in a more thorough way than many of his contemporaries. His declaration that "It is ridiculous to play the flute in a land where the national instrument is the powerful *assotor* drum" is eloquent testimony to his ideological bent. He went on to reject the later Marxist leanings of *indigenisme* as too intellectual and became aggressively afrocentric in his defense of the ideology of *noirisme* in the pages of the magazine *Les Griots* (1938–1940). At this time, the early eroticism and populism in his writing give way to a strident apology for authoritarian politics based on racial authenticity. From the 1940s a remarkable change became apparent in his work as he rejected all his Africanist ideas and preoccupations with vaudou for a mystical Catholicism and a reverence for French cultural traditions.

Jacques Roumain (1907–1944) is undoubtedly the most important writer to emerge in post-occupation Haiti. He was the first Haitian writer to achieve international recognition, with the novel that exemplified the best elements of Haitian *indigenisme* and marked the coming of age of the peasant novel, *Gouverneurs de la rosée* (Masters of the dew). His reputation rests on this novel, which was translated into more than a dozen languages and adapted for the stage and the cinema. He also dominated local politics with his fierce anti-U.S. sentiment in the 1920s and his creation of the Haitian Communist Party in 1934.

More cosmopolitan than his contemporaries—who, like him, were born into the Haitian elite and spent some of their formative years in Europe—he saw himself both as an activist for the promotion of the culture of the

Haitian masses and as an international figure who would link Haitian nationalism to similar movements in the rest of the Caribbean, black North America, and South America. Seen as too subversive because of his strong communist ties, he was sent into exile, after a short prison term, in 1934. He traveled widely in leftist circles at this time and established close contact with such international Marxist writers as Langston Hughes, Pablo Neruda, and Nicolas Guillen. He returned to Haiti in 1941 and immediately got involved in local politics with his public criticism of the Catholic Church's campaign to rid Haiti of vaudou. The years in exile establish Roumain both as an insightful polemicist and as a keen observer of culture and politics. His *Analyse schématique* (Schematic analysis) in 1934 was the first Marxist analysis of the failings of Haitian society. Equally insightful were his analysis of lynching in the plantation South, *Les griefs de l'homme noir* (The black man's grievances, 1939) and his examination of peasant religion as a function of material circumstances in *Autour de la campagne anti-superstitieuse* (Concerning the anti-superstitious campaign, 1943).

During his militant early years, his writing, oddly enough, consisted of mostly stylized mood poems evoking landscape of personal states of mind. His first prose works were short stories that were either bleak satires of the Haitian elite, *Les fantoches* (The puppets) in 1930 and *La proie et l'ombre* (The prey and its shadow) in 1931, or an equally bleak peasant novella, *La montagne ensorcelée* (The enchanted mountain, 1931). Roumain's best-known mature work consisted of sweeping calls to proletarian revolt. The epic poems of the collection *Bois d'Ebène* (Ebony Wood) are thundering appeals for working class solidarity. The novel *Gouverneurs de la rosée* was written very much in the utopian spirit of these later works, while Roumain was Haitian chargé d'affaires in Mexico, and published posthumously. Roumain's major achievement was as much a politically motivated parable of the hardships of rural Haiti as an anthropologically accurate picture of peasant culture. The novel goes beyond the "indigeniste" tendency to blindly glorify Haitian popular religion. The plot evokes a utopian vision of worker solidarity and a renewal of culture through collective labor, which is preached to the villagers of Fonds Rouge by the protagonist, Manuel, who returns to his divided, drought-stricken village after cutting cane in Cuba. More than just another orthodox Marxist work, Roumain's narrative presents a moving poetic universe and a mythic tale of human self-sacrifice.

Roumain's leftism had little effect on his contemporaries, who were more preoccupied with the racial folk values, religious mysticism, and organic notions of culture. Nor was his novel seen as particularly dangerous by Haiti's political establishment. In the wake of *indigenisme*, cultural authenticity became the hallmark of thought and writing in the 1930s and 1940s under the profound influence of the ethnologist Jean Price-Mars. One of Haiti's foremost intellectuals, Price-Mars (1876–1969) exercised as much influence at home during the U.S. occupation as he did on the negritude movement in Paris in the 1930s. His early work was concerned with educational reform in Haiti, but he soon became known for his criticism of the elite in his 1919 book, *La vocation de L'élite* (The elite's responsibility), which was intensified in his deservedly famous ethnological study of Haitian culture, *Ainsi parla l'oncle* (So spoke the uncle, 1928). In this work, which first appeared as a series of lectures, Price-Mars criticized the Haitian elite for their *bovarysme collectif*, or their excessively francophile attitudes. More importantly, however, this book was a defense and illustration of Haitian peasant culture, language, and religion and a celebration of Haiti's African heritage. He was a key figure in the cultural politics of the post-occupation period, which saw the rise of the noiriste movement in the 1930s.

The U.S. occupation had forced Haitians to recognize that their nation was culturally heterogeneous and that for too long the African elements in Haitian culture had been seen as unworthy. This sense of Haiti's dual heritage was so pervasive at the time that even writers who were not part of any particular ideological orientation felt compelled to address this question. Indeed, one of the best-known poems on the question of cultural duality is Léon Laleau's "Trahison," which appeared in his 1931 book of poems, *Musique nègre* (Black music) in which he lamented the fact that the Haitian soul was torn between "Des sentiments d'emprunt et des coutumes / D'Europe" and "Ce Coeur qui m'est venu du Sénégal" (Borrowed feelings and habits / from Europe and This heart that has come to me from Senegal). With *noirisme*, race—which had essentially been an intellectual issue up to then— hardened into a rigid ideological position that extolled the virtues of the black soul, dwelt on the idea of black victimization and mulatto racism, and argued for Haiti to turn to a politics of racial authenticity. These extremist views, which were fed by the excesses of the mulatto presidents in the post-occupation period, were disseminated in the magazine *Les Griots*, which counted as one of its founders Francois Duvalier, who would turn *noirisme* into the state ideology when he came to power in 1957. As Duvalier himself, along with his fellow collaborator Lorimer Denis, declared in his description of the Griot doctrine, "All our efforts from independence to today have concentrated on the systematic repression of our African heritage both in literary and in socio-political matters, our actions must now lead us to a revaluation of this racial factor."

The literary production of the noiriste movement was largely centered on

Carl Brouard, with his increasingly frenzied portrayals of vaudou possession and erotic fantasy. By the 1940s Brouard had begun his final descent into incoherence, and this seemed to signal the end of a noiriste poetics based on racial mysticism; the whole ethnological movement in Haiti remained an entirely local issue, spawned in the wake of the U.S. occupation. By the 1950s, however, the negritude movement, headquartered in Paris and pan-African in scope, would draw Haitian identity politics into the mainstream of the ideals of a neo-African diaspora. Negritude, with its insistence on Africanist cultural retentions and its strident appeals for decolonization, seemed to both legitimize the politics of Haitian *noirisme* and to spread a noiriste poetics beyond the Griot movement. This international movement also gave Haitian writers a new sense of translinguitic and transnational solidarity with black writers all over the world. As the French Existentialist Jean-Paul Sartre declared in his 1948 introduction to the first anthology of the new black poetry by Leopold Sedar Senghor, "From Haiti to Cayenne, one single aim: to express the black soul."[1]

One effect of this new international movement on Haitian writing would be a new uniformity in theme and style in Haitian poetry. The extravagance and originality of Carl Brouard was quickly replaced by a repetitive new verse imitating the themes of black solidarity and racial revenge launched by the fathers of the negritude movement, Aimé Cesaire, Léopold Sédar Senghor, and Léon Damas. A rigid decorum was now apparent in Haitian poetry, where poets such as Roussan Camille, René Bélance, Regnor Bernard, and Jean Brierre turned out a stream of epic poems excoriating the nightmare of colonialism and heralding the dawn of violent racial rebirth. The best known and most frequently anthologized of this group on writers is undoubtedly Jean Brierre (1909–1992). Brierre played an active role in the nationalist backlash against the occupation and established his reputation early as a writer of politically committed, dramatic verse. He studied for a while at Columbia University in New York and was later noted for his celebratory tributes to such African American artists as Langston Hughes, Paul Robeson, and Marian Anderson. His best-known epic poem, written in the manner of Haitian negritude, was *Black Soul* (1947). Written in free verse and lamenting the universal suffering of the black race, it ultimately and, perhaps predictably, heralds at the end a new dawn of racial pride as Brierre envisages racial redemption in terms of a world that will ultimately notice that black hands *"ont laissé aux murs de la Civilisation / des empreintes d'amour, de grace et de lumière"* (have left on the walls of Civilization / the imprints of love, grace, and light).

POSTWAR WRITING

In the period following World War II a new openness became evident in Haiti's intellectual and artistic life. No longer simply a deviant and hostile society, Haiti became better known to the outside world because of the discovery of Haitian primitive art by Dewitt Peters and the publication of important anthropological studies of Haiti by Melville Herskovits, Harold Courlander, and James Leyburn. An influential American critic, Edmund Wilson, recorded impressions of his visit to Haiti in *Red, Black, Blond, and Olive* (1956), and the novel *Canapé Vert* by Philippe and Pierre Thoby Marcelin won the prize for the best novel from Latin America in a contest sponsored by the Pan-American Union. A number of important literary figures also visited Haiti at this time, including such Caribbean artists as Wifredo Lam, Aimé Cesaire, Nicolas Guillén, and Alejo Carpentier, many of whom were friends of Jacques Roumain. Poet René Depestre, a key figure from the postwar generation, described the impact of this new internationalism in the following ways:

> Before the war, Haiti was shut in on its own misery. You could never imagine the extent to which we suffered from cultural insularity, surrounded on all sides by lies. Men like Guillen, Carpentier, Césaire, Langston Hughes, Pierre Mabille, Louis Jouvet, Wifredo Lam, André Breton, really who could, better than they, provide wonderful new perspectives for our youthful imaginations?[2]

What many of these visitors to Haiti also had in common was a link of one kind or another with the surrealist movement. In particular, surgeon and art critic Pierre Mabille, who had been active in the French surrealist movement since the 1930s and who had been appointed French cultural attaché and director of the French Institute in Port-au-Prince in 1945, was enormously influential in promoting the ideals of surrealism among aspiring Haitian writers, especially the young Depestre and his contemporary, Jacques Stephen Alexis. The interest of Mabille in Haiti was as much artistic as anthropological and political. He became seriously interested in vaudou and taught at Roumain's Institute of Ethnology, and his most important single gesture was to invite his old friend André Breton to do a short lecture series in Haiti, which would coincide with an exhibition of paintings by Wifredo Lam in 1945.

Breton's lectures had unexpected results. The literary as well as political history of Haiti would not have been the same had he not unleashed a powerful revolutionary idealism among young Haitians by articulating the ideals of surrealism. The generation of Depestre and Alexis, who were the founders of the militant student newspaper *La Ruche*, felt a great affinity with surrealism and its critique of the repressive values of the West. They devoted a special edition of the newspaper to Breton in which they called for a general insurrection. A national strike followed and the then president, Elie Lescot, was forced from office in 1946. These were heady days for the students of *La Ruche*, who were now living a surrealist revolution that emphasized the bond between political activist and creative writer. For the next few decades Haitian literature would be dominated by Alexis and Depestre, the ideals of the surrealist revolution of 1946, and increasing conflict between the radical writer and the repressive state.

Jacques Stephen Alexis (1922–1961) was born during the U.S. occupation and traveled extensively with his father, the diplomat and novelist Stephen Alexis. He was influenced from an early time by the Marxist ideals of Jacques Roumain and later by André Breton and the theory of "marvellous realism" proposed by the Cuban novelist Alejo Carpentier. He regularly wrote a column for *La Ruche*, which he signed Jacques La Colère. After studying neurology in Paris he returned to Haiti, where he wrote his major works, a series of dense lyrical novels dealing with Haitian history, popular culture, and the folk imagination. Like those of his mentor Alejo Carpentier, his narratives are imaginative re-creations of Haitian history. Following in the footsteps of Jacques Roumain, he wrote about the emergence of a political *prise de conscience* among the Haitian masses. He came to prominence in 1956 when he challenged the monolithic theory of negritude by presenting a paper on the "Marvelous Realism of Haitians" at the First Congress of Black Writers in Paris. His left-wing Part d'Entente Populaire challenged Duvalier in the early years of his presidency. He was later killed by Duvalier's militia, which was attempting to invade Haiti clandestinely in 1961.

Alexis' novels focus on the urban poor. His first work, *Compère général soleil* (General Br'er Sun, 1955), is set in the teeming slums of Port-au-Prince and is tied to the massacre of Haitian cane cutters in the Dominican Republic in 1937. Despite the somber events depicted, the novel concentrates on the epileptic hero, who is ostracized because of his illness, becomes politicized in prison, and goes to the Dominican Republic to seek work. His political activism there costs him his life, but the rising sun of revolutionary faith suggested in the title brings the novel to an idealistic close. In a similar vein, his 1957 novel, *Les arbres musiciens* (The musician trees), documents the effects of the anti-superstitious campaign waged by the Catholic Church under President Lescot. He shifts from the grand historical-social frescoes of his two early novels to a less conventionally historical one in two later works that take greater liberties with the novel form and are more closely tied to his theory of marvellous realism. *L'espace d'un cillement* (The twinkling of an eye, 1959) is not constrained by historical circumstance and is a symbolic encounter between a Dominican prostitute and a Cuban mechanic in a Haitian brothel. In a similarly imaginative way, his last published work, *Romancero aux étoiles* (A serenade to the stars, 1960), integrates his own fiction with traditional Haitian folktales. Like his entire *oeuvre*, these tales evoke the Haitian people's imaginative response to their history of uprooting, repression, and misery.

René Depestre was born in 1926 and had very much the same literary and ideological influences as Alexis. After the events of 1946, he too went to study in Paris and was drawn to the nationalist ideas of the French poet Louis Aragon. This was the beginning of a nomadic life for Depestre, who spent three years in Latin America before returning to Haiti in 1957. Threatened by Duvalier's regime, he left in 1959 for Cuba, where Castro's regime had just come to power. Eventually, at odds with the Cuban government, he left in 1979 to work for UNESCO in Paris and has lived in the south of France since his retirement in 1986.

Depestre's first collections of poetry, *Etincelles* (Sparks, 1945) and *Gerbe de sang* (Spray of blood, 1946), were exuberant celebrations of youthful revolt and influenced by the French Resistance poets, Paul Eluard and Louis Aragon. The political verse written in Europe in the 1950s were little more than Marxists tracts. However, the later poems, especially *Minerai noir* (Black ore) in 1956 and *Journal d'un animal marin* (Journal of a sea creature) in 1964 reveal a fuller range of themes, from lyrical love poems to wry evocations of exile. Anti-U.S. politics and celebrations of Cuban socialism became apparent in books of poetry written during Depestre's years in Cuba, *Un arc en ciel pour l'Occident Chrétien* (A rainbow for the Christian West, 1967) and *Poète à Cuba* (Poet in Cuba, 1976). During these years Depestre's critique of negritude and its Haitian variant, *noirisme*, became more explicit. Depestre's theoretical writing was later published in the tellingly entitled *Bonjour et adieu à la negritude* (Hello and goodbye to negritude, 1980). At this time he also shifted his attention to fiction, which did not always meet the approval of his Cuban hosts. The short stories in *Alleluia pour une femme jardin* (Alleluia for a garden woman) in 1973 turned away from political protest to celebrate the theme of erotic adventure. Similarly, the anti-Duvalierist *roman à clef, Le mat de cocagne* (The greasy pole, 1979), associates political dictatorship with sexual repression and promotes the vaudou religion as a source of sexual liberation. These prose works mark a shift from the Marxist

phase in Depestre's verse to a single-minded concentration on his early surrealist interests. Global eroticism and the pleasures of exile are the hallmarks
of his most recent work. Depestre assiduously avoids comment on the current
political situation in Haiti. *Hadriana dans tous mes rêves* (Hadriana in all my
dreams), written in the tradition of marvelous realism, was awarded the Prix
Renaudot in 1988. It is the first of an erotic trilogy, the second of which,
Eros dans un train chinois (Eros in a Chinese train), was published in 1990.

The Duvalier presidency brought literature inspired by radical politics to
an abrupt end in Haiti. The last echoes of this tradition were found in the
short-lived movement attached to the magazine *Haiti Littéraire*, (Literary
Haiti) in which poets such as Anthony Phelps and René Philoctète argued
for broad humanist ideals for Haitian literature. Such writing could exist
only in exile communities, which were quickly being created as writers and
intellectuals were forced out of Haiti or voluntarily fled Duvalier's reign of
terror. The Nouvelle Optique group, based in Montreal and directed by
Herard Jadotte, published a journal by the same name in the 1970s and
many novels whose sole purpose was to denounce Duvalierism. This subgenre
of politically committed fiction was used to exorcise painful memories and
like all *littérature de circonstance*, would not outlast the political circumstances
that gave it birth. The best examples of this strident anti-Duvalierist novel
of protest are the early novels of Gerard Etienne, *Le nègre crucifie, récit* (The
crucified black man, a narrative, 1974) and *Un ambassadeur macoute à Montreal* (A macoute ambassador in Montreal, 1979), published with *La Nouvelle
Optique*. In these works Etienne is obsessed with the tortured bodies of black
victims, and in the 1979 novel the Montreal authorities import one of Duvalier's Macoutes to put down unrest in the Canadian city. Sometimes this
preoccupation with the land left behind led to rather sentimental portraits
of home in novels that were invariably set in the countryside and contained
stock characters. One can find examples of this kind of exoticism in such
works by the Paris-based writer, Jean Métellus, as *Jacmel au crepuscule* (Jacmel
at twilight, 1981) and *La famille Vortex* (The Vortex family, 1982). Novels
of this kind enjoyed a certain amount of popularity among foreign readers
who tend to be drawn to the quaint aspects of Haitian society and culture.
However, twenty-nine years of Duvalierism would change Haitian society
and culture profoundly and irrevocably as well as undermine the Haitian
writers' ability to relate to this changed world. These transformations would
make novels of local color as well as novels of protest anachronistic to an
informed readership.

DUVALIER AND AFTER

The Duvalier dynasty began in 1957 and lasted twenty-nine years. In literary and cultural terms, it meant the coming of age of the noiriste movement in Haiti. Evidence of the need to create cultural symbols was widespread in Haiti in the 1960s. The erection of a statue to the unknown maroon in the Champ de Mars, the changing of the Haitian flag from red and blue to red and black, the visit of Haile Selassie, and the naming of a major street in Port-au-Prince after Martin Luther King, Jr., were some of the symbolic acts that were motivated by a noiriste ideology. Duvalierism was portrayed as the culmination of a process begun by the maroons and Dessalines. There was much intellectual investment in this tendentious reading of Haitian history, which portrayed black leaders as more nationalistic than their mulatto counterparts. The excesses of this creation of a legendary black past actually provoked a response from the man who was considered the father of Haitian *noirisme*, Jean Price-Mars. In 1967 Price-Mars wrote an open letter to the then noiriste dean of the Faculty of Arts at the State University, criticizing the latter's excessive emphasis on the issue of race in his interpretation of Haitian history and culture. Ostracism came swiftly as Price-Mars was publicly vilified for challenging official state policy.

This incident is a striking example of the way in which noiriste ideology had not only become adopted as official state ideology but had also grown intolerant of any opposition, even from those who were considered formative influences on the movement. The Duvalierist credo was voiced by spokesmen like René Piquion, who constantly echoed Duvalier's opposition to the "atheist materialism" of Marxism and his assertion that Haiti did not have anything to learn from foreign ideologies. Duvalier's own writings were collected in his *Oeuvres essentielles* (Essential works), whose very title suggested that they represented the final word on all subjects. Not surprisingly, there is little evidence of any independent literary or cultural movement in Haiti at the time. The only literary school worthy of such a name is *spiralisme*, which was founded by Franck Etienne along with his contemporaries, the poet René Philoctète and the critic Jean Claude Fignolé.

Franck Etienne was the only member of the group who attempted to elaborate the ideas of *spiralisme* in his work. A mathematician by training, Franck Etienne used the model of the open-ended spiral—both in opposition to the closed, authoritarian discourse of Duvalierism and in order to elaborate a new experimental form in the Haitian novel. Never openly political, his prose fiction was always characterized by complex narrative perspective and a mystical sense of the link between spirituality and matter. After a few books of poetry, his first major work was the novel *Mûr à crever* (Ripe for bursting, 1968), which uses a "spiraliste" style to evoke the frustrations of the generation of the 1960s under Duvalier. In an attempt to break from the heroic socialist realism that marked earlier Haitian fiction, he produced *Ultravocal* (Beyond voicing) in 1972, which was an even more entangled, polyphonic narrative form that crossed genres and mixed realism and fantasy in narrating the fortunes of Marc Arbre, the incarnation of evil, and Vatel, a man condemned to wandering. Etienne's most famous work was written in Creole, *Dezafi* (Defiance, 1975) and can be read as his most overt political allegory. In this novel the people of the village of Bois Neuf are zombified by a tyrannical houngan, or vaudou priest. Salt is used in the story to liberate them from their lethargy and to bring them to full consciousness. The ensuring revolt foreshadows the movement of popular revolt that would overthrow the Duvalier regime approximately ten years later. After the success of this novel, Etienne turned to painting and the theatre, where he enjoyed success with a number of plays in Creole, of which *Pelin-Tet* (Head traps, 1978), an original adaptation of *Les Émigrés* by Slamowir Mrozek, is the best known.

The other major literary figure who wrote from within Haiti and experienced the oppression of the Duvalierist state directly was rather different from Etienne. Marie Chauvet, who began in the theatre and then turned to the novel, is the most important female novelist from Haiti. In the late 1950s and early 1960s she wrote three novels, which though accomplished were essentially reworkings of the well-established genres of historical fiction and the peasant novel. Her reputation is based on the 1968 trilogy *Amour colère folie* (Love, anger, madness), which was attacked on its publication because of its not-so-subtle critique of Duvalierism and its portrayal of the elite as corrupt and decadent. Chauvet's first and best-known story in the trilogy is "Amour." Like "Colère" and "Folie," which evoke the transformation of human beings to an animal-like state under violent police oppression, "Amour" is shocking in its exploration of the workings of the terrorist state. However, this story also examines more fully the psychology of the individual within such a state in an attempt to explain the strange complicity that could exist between the victims of oppression and the oppressors. The story is told in a diary written by an unmarried woman, Claire, who lives in a provincial town and is from a dispossessed elite family. She is a misfit because of her tormented mental and unmarried state as well as her growing reaction to the brutalities of the regime and the hypocrisy of her class. She is drawn to her brother-in-law, a Frenchman, and initially indulges in a voyeuristic existence, spying on him and attempting to manipulate him away from her sister. Her obsession shifts from her sister's husband to the police chief, who has subjected the town to a reign of terror. She hates him but is drawn to him. She eventually kills him in an ambiguous act that does not liberate her but seems to push her further into claustrophobic confinement. Chauvet's fictional trilogy quickly disappeared from circulation and has never been reprinted. She died in exile in the United States in 1973 without publishing another work.

Outside Haiti, writers were naturally freer to express themselves. Even though this group, which became known as the Haitian diaspora, never produced a major novel on the Duvalier dictatorship, exile meant a new lease on life for experimentation with the novel, a broadening of the sphere of experience, and the emergence of theatre. Haitian literature was no longer routinely set in Haiti and even saw the production of novels that had nothing to do with Haiti, such as *La parole prisonnière* (The imprisoned word, 1986) by Jean Métellus. Poetry received relatively little creative attention at this time, and the only major voice to express the anxieties and opportunities of exile is the poet Anthony Phelps, who lived in Canada during the Duvalier years. Even Phelps, however, is known for the novel *Mémoire en colin maillard* (Memory and blind man's buff, 1976), which is a dreamlike evocation of the day-to-day horrors of life under Duvalierism.

Conditions for novelists of the Haitian diaspora differed greatly from their counterparts within Haiti and from their literary predecessors. They were not only free of political censorship, they could also benefit from more creative literary environments in the many cities in which they invariably settled. They were exposed to a more literate and demanding readership and could, through journals such as *Nouvelle Optique* and *Collectif Paroles* in Canada, participate quite fully in intellectual debates on Haitian writing in particular and in new literary trends as a whole. It is therefore not surprising that there has been an increasing sophistication in fiction produced outside Haiti, which has become the new creative site for Haitian writing.

Novels written outside Haiti fall broadly into two categories thematically and stylistically. On the one hand, there are novels that remain attached to a Haitian setting and characters. The most creative of these novels use a style that could be loosely categorized as marvelous realism to describe the puzzling events in a world that eludes realistic depiction. On the other hand, there are those works of fiction that are more driven to challenge, often irreverently, notions of folk, belonging, and identity as defined by Haitian noiriste ideologues. These novels are set outside Haiti and follow the intellectual and geographical wanderings of the narrator. Sometimes writing in the first category fell prey to prevailing literary trends and shrewdly exploited the vogue of marvelous realism, which collapsed the distinction between dream and reality. Rene Depestre's *Hadriana dans tous mes rêves* is just such a colorful and humorous chronicle of tropical sensuality in which a young woman from a respectable family is turned into a zombie. Even though less successful than Depestre's novel, another work in this vein is Jean Claude Fignolé's *Les possédés de la pleine lune* (Those possessed by the full moon, 1987), whose title suggests the book's major themes of mystery and possession in rural Haiti. Even though Fignolé never lived in exile, he has a sense of market trends, which blur the distinction between writers on the inside and writers on the outside.

The most original practitioners of this late phase of Haitian marvelous realism steered clear of the clichéd evocation of the Haitian countryside. In this regard, Pierre Clitandre's proletarian novel, *Cathédrale du mois d'août* (Cathedral of the month of August, 1980), takes place in the slums of Port-au-Prince and is a striking example of the depiction of the spectacle of destitution of Haiti's urban shanty town. Another remarkable novelist who departs from a narrow definition of literary realism in his work is Emile Ollivier, who has lived in Canada since the mid-1960s. In a number of successful works of fiction he tackles the enigmatic question of the transformation of Duvalier's Haiti and the impossibility of returning to one's native land. His first success was with *Mère-Solitude* (Mother-Solitude, 1983), in which the protagonist's search for his mother, who was publicly executed in Haiti, evoked details of the Haiti's capital, Haitian history, and the horrors of Duvalierism in such an allusive and private way that it was difficult for foreign readers to grasp. Ollivier's novels are neither trendy nor facile. He obviously uses the freedom and the distance afforded by exile to scrutinize more carefully the issue of displacement in the modern world. His second work, *Passages* (1991) again using a complicated narrative structure, was more accessible to a foreign audience. It treated the phenomenon of Haitian exile in terms of the intersecting lives of a poor woman who ends up in Florida as one of the Haitian boat people and an exiled militant intellectual. His most recent novel, *Les urnes scellées* (The sealed ballots, 1995), again looks at the question of departure and return. In this instance, the main character, after many years of exile in Canada, decides to return to an unnamed island, which looks strikingly like Haiti after the fall of Duvalier. He is an archaeologist who now discovers that exhuming the truth in the present is as difficult as it is for lost civilizations. He witnesses the drive-by shooting of a distant relative on election day and tries to solve this murder. He is thrown into a futile quest that leaves him puzzled by the barbarity as well as the joie de vivre of a society to which he feels he can no longer belong. The novel plays on the French word *urne*, which can mean both "ballot box" and "funeral urn." The protagonist's experience of the barbarity of the election

means the death of his link with his homeland. He leaves even more per-
plexed than when he first arrived.

The second group of novelists tend to set their narratives outside Haiti and
perhaps take the anxieties over exile, alienation, and self-definition of the Haitian migrant further than the generally older novelists, who are preoccupied
by impossible returns. In the second group, Jean Claude Charles and Dany
Laferrière were among the first to successfully set their novels outside Haiti.
In the case of the former, the heroes of his novels work for the international
press and are more likely to be found in Manhattan hotel rooms, the Left
Bank in Paris, or in a jazz club in Greenwich Village than attending a vaudou
ceremony in Jacmel. Novels such as *Manhattan Blues* (1985) and *Ferdinand
je suis à Paris* (Ferdinand I am in Paris, 1987), published by Charles in Paris,
cannot be narrowly defined as Haitian. The protagonists, shared by both
these novels, are admittedly Haitian, but they exist in an international environment that is as far as one could get from Creole, vaudou, and Duvalierist
terror. One is more likely to find English phrases than Creole expressions in
these novels, which recount the adventures of characters who are essentially
flâneurs (wanderers) in Old and New World metropolises.

The multilingual and interracial environment of Charles's novels recurs in
a far more irreverent way in the work of Dany Laferrière, who like Charles
is more likely to be influenced by culture and literature outside Haiti than
by specifically national concerns. Laferrière, also a journalist like Charles,
achieved instant notoriety with his 1985 novel *Comment faire l'amour avec
un nègre sans se fatiguer* (How to make love with a negro without getting
tired). Not only is this episodic narrative set in the bohemian student quarters
of Montreal, it is explicit in its treatment of sexuality, which is generally
absent from Haitian writing. It does not once mention Haiti but is set in a
filthy room where the two protagonists listen to jazz, read a range of books
from the Koran to Henry Miller's erotic novels, and have frequent sex with
Canadian women with names like Ms. Literature and Ms. Snob. This novel
has been scandalously successful because of its outrageous satire of sexual
stereotypes, both male and female, black and white. It was translated into
English and made into a film with the prudishly abridged title *How to Make
Love . . .* in 1990.

More important, the raw, freewheeling prose of this novel calls into to
question the major received ideas of Haitian literature: the value of cultural
rootedness, the importance of the book, and the verbal eloquence normally
associated with Haitian literature. Laferrière willfully mocks some of the more
sensitive racial questions associated with black literature and black writers.
His early novel bristles with such statements as: "It is true that the West has

plundered Africa but this black can read" and "One is not born black, one becomes black." It also tackles directly the ambiguities of the Haitian writer, who can no longer see himself as simply displaced but part of an international community of migrant writers in large metropolitan cities. Laferrière's characters are black and francophone and have intimate relations with women from the white anglophone world. Similarly, they read texts in English but continue to express themselves in French. Ultimately, Laferrière's novel is about writing—or, more specifically, about a man writing a novel and, in its own provoking way, a kind of literary manifesto. The main character, anonymously called Man, is writing his experiences down in a novel, which seems to bring to an end many of the grandiose claims made for Haitian literature.

In this work, filled with ambiguities, which could only be described as post-modern, Laferrière claims an unprecedented freedom for the Haitian writer, who is no longer expected to continue a tradition that ideologically and aesthetically goes back to the nineteenth century. This is not an idiosyncratic act of provocation but the voice of a new generation of Haitian writers. In the novels that have followed his initial success, Laferrière has continued to explore the paths opened by his first literary success. Two of his subsequent major novels are *Cette grenade dans la main du jeune nègre est-elle une arme ou un fruit?* (This grenade/grenadine in the young black man's hand, is it a weapon or a fruit?) in 1993 and *Pays sans chapeau* (Land without a hat) in 1996. They are both rather original travel books. In the first instance the United States is the site for the narrator's journey, and in the second Laferrière recounts his return to Haiti. Both can be read as sequels to that initial evocation of the writer as wanderer across cultures, as much at home in the United States, where he encounters the vaudou goddess Erzulie in the shape of the pop star Madonna, and at a loss in the face of the chaotic images of today's Haiti. They both also continue Laferrière's concern with devising a new style of writing: less literary, more suited to television, and more interactively oral.

In clearing a new space, both aesthetically and ideologically, for the Haitian writer abroad, Laferrière ushers in the possibility of even more radical forms of writing, which we may have some difficulty defining as Haitian. The related issues of displacement, autobiography, and language make Laferrière's literary irreverence pivotal to what appears to be the next phase of Haitian writing. In this new phase, Haitian writers will further problematize the issue of national identity by writing in English as well as projecting images of traditional Haiti as unjust and constricting, especially in the case of women. The current success of Edwidge Danticat is the best example we have of a new voice in Haitian writing. Writing exclusively in English, Dandicat joins other female writers from the Caribbean like Christina Garcia and Julia Alvarez, who write in English about the experience of belonging both to the United States and the Caribbean. Journey in Danticat's novel is not about the anxieties of dislocation but about liberation from gender stereotypes and awakening to new kinds of self-fulfillment. In her first novel, *Breath, Eyes, Memory* (1994), which was enthusiastically received, Danticat explores the relations between three generations of Haitian women who become increasingly involved with the United States.

It is not too farfetched to see in the plot of this novel a symbolic representation of a shift in values from the oppressively parochial and patriarchal world of Haiti to the liberating anonymity of the large American city. The narrator's father is a Macoute who has raped her mother and abandoned her. The victim of the rape then leaves the unwanted child with her grandmother and migrates to the United States. The child eventually joins her mother in the United States, and the novel ends with the narrator, who herself is now a mother, taking the dead body of her mother back to Haiti for burial. The main theme of the story is tied to the construction of gender in Haiti, the fetishizing of virginity, and the sexual liberation of the narrator outside her oppressive native land. The narrator's mother, who has been both politically and sexually victimized, inflicts on her daughter a kind of victimization because of her obsession with her daughter's virginity. Liberation means ultimately a defiance of sexual taboo. Even though there has been some interesting new work by contemporary Haitian female writers, such as Jan Dominique's exploration of mental breakdown in *Mémoire d'une amnesique* (Memoir of an amnesiac, 1984), and the fashionably feminist *Les chemins de loco-miroir* (The ways of reflecting loco, 1990) by Lilas Desquiron, Danticat seems the most strikingly original of current female writers.

In her recent novel, *The Farming of Bones* (1998), Danticat both rewrites the heroic, historical novel *Compère général soleil* (General Br'er Sun), written by Jacques Stephen Alexis about the massacre of Haitian cane cutters in the Dominican Republic, and recounts a tale of emotional awakening in another zone of cultural indeterminacy, the border between Haiti and the Dominican Republic. Though never overtly political, Danticat's work does not shy away from the brutal reality of the lives of ordinary Haitians, whether the fate of boat people or in this novel, which recaptures one of the more disturbing episodes of Haitian history. Her aim, however, is not simply to recount the past or to lay blame. Rather, she is more interested in the psychological growth of her characters because of displacement. In *The Farming of Bones* the narrator and protagonist is of Haitian origin but has always lived comfortably in the Dominican Republic, where she was adopted by a Dominican family after her parents' drowning. She becomes romantically involved with an itinerant worker who seems capable of restoring the emotional links with a country that were severed when her parents drowned. Ethnic cleansing in her land of adoption puts an end to this possibility, and she loses all her sources of emotional security and ends up in a refugee camp. This novel warns of the brutal excesses of blind nationalism, but like Danticat's earlier work it is also an investment in the narrator's ability to transcend the past. The novel ends with the protagonist in the same river where her parents drowned and where the caneworkers were massacred, awaiting the dawn with expectation.

WRITING IN CREOLE

No account of Haitian literature can be complete without a discussion of writing in Creole. As we have seen, the Haitian elite generally adopted a fetishistic attitude to the French language and despised Creole either as the inferior tongue of illiterate peasants and common laborers or at best as a quaint variation of standard French. The fact that almost 90 percent of the Haitian population is made up of monolingual Creole speakers means that this language cannot be easily dismissed. The present Haitian constitution considers both French and Creole as official languages. It is, therefore, not surprising that the nationalistic movements beginning in the nineteenth century with Oswald Durand's "Choucoune" and *Cric-Crac*, the translation of La Fontaine's *Fables* into Creole by Georges Sylvain, have sought to counter the stigma attached to the language of the Haitian masses. This has been particularly so since the U.S. occupation, during which a more anti-establishment and ethnocentric nationalism insisted with increasing stridency on a rejection of French cultural models and on the use of Creole in literary texts. Creole has consequently become a sign of linguistic authenticity for many, proof of African retentions for others, and the true language of the masses for those who are driven by populist ideologies. Literary movements, which valued an improvised, spoken style, and genres like the theatre, which depend on dramatic performance, also championed the Creole folk tale and the literary use of Creole because it is mainly an oral language.

It is therefore not surprising that the writing genre least favored in Creole is the novel. Not only is the purely literary use of Creole problematic, but the novel form is dominated by writers from the diaspora. The list of prose fiction in Creole is, consequently, quite short, and in those instances where novels in Creole have been successfully written, the authors have felt compelled to do French versions of their prose narratives. For example, Frank Etienne felt compelled to publish a French version of his Creole novel *Dezafi* (1975) four years after its publication. *Les affres d'un défi* (Defiance and dread) appeared in 1979 and was perhaps more read than the original. Similarly, Felix Morisseau-Leroy, better known as a playwright and poet, published his collection of tales, *Ravinodyab* (La Ravine aux diables [The devils' gully]) in 1982 in a bilingual edition. Creole has quite often been used in Haitian fiction to give some sense of place and local color. The most successful experiment in this combination of Creole and French is Jacques Roumain's critically acclaimed novel, *Gouverneurs de la rosée*. In this case, the Indigenous movement's desire for literary authenticity necessitated the use of Creole proverbs, colloquial expressions, and a more oral inflection in the French narrative. However, Roumain felt obliged to provide a glossary in French and to retain the use of French syntax in the Creole-inflected dialogue spoken by his peasants.

Far more promising genres for the use of Creole are poetry and the theatre. In this regard, the outstanding practitioners are undoubtedly Frank Etienne and the late Felix Morisseau-Leroy (1912–1998). Morisseau-Leroy is a pivotal figure in the promotion of the literary use of Creole because of his Creole production of Sophocles' *Antigone* in 1953. Morisseau-Leroy's adaptation drew parallels between Creon's oppressive rule in Thebes and political absolutism in Haiti. Set in a Haitian village, the play related the Greek themes of civil war, the curse of the gods, and explosive personal animosities to Haitian politics. The dramatist also used storytelling conventions to provide even more credibility to this reconstructed Greek fable. The Haitian audience easily identified with the test of wills between the weak, Antigone, and the strong, Creon, who is played as a ruthless vaudou priest who has the backing of the state. In this play, Morisseau-Leroy demonstrated that Creole could be used to depict serious political issues and not just light comedy, as had been the habit in the past. The play was enthusiastically received as the first successful attempt to translate a classical work into the language of the Haitian masses. In the same year, Morisseau-Leroy published his collection of Creole poems, *Diacoute*, which were later recorded. Again his writing is highly politicized and cleverly exploits the dramatic potential of spoken Creole.

Antigone seemed to anticipate the rise of Duvalierism, and two years after Francois Duvailer took power in 1957, Morisseau-Leroy left Haiti for exile, most of which he spent in Senegal, Ghana, and Florida. His later work never achieved the same success as his Creole experiments in the early 1950s. He returned to the theme of political dictatorship in his *Roi Créon* (King Creon), which was also written in Creole and directly referred to Duvalier's brutal regime. This play is little different, however, from the stream of Duvalier writing we find in the 1970s in the Haitian diaspora. Theatre in the Creole language in the Duvalier period is dominated by Franck Etienne—or Franketienne, as he renamed himself. Etienne's concept of *spiralisme* was at least as well suited to the theatre as it was to the novel. In the mid-1970s Etienne turned away from prose fiction to writing in Creole for the theatre. His theatre was as interactive as the spiraliste model suggests, between dream and reality, actors and audience. His career as a dramatist could develop in the 1970s and 1980s because the regime of Jean Claude Duvalier was more liberal that that of his father.

His first play, *Trouforban*, in 1978, whose title refers to a place that is suspiciously like Duvalier's Haiti, is about the sacrifices that are required by a diabolical character called Sarazin. The same interest in politics can be found in such plays as *Bobomasouri* (The smile of evil, 1984) inspired by the absurdist drama of Samuel Beckett, and *Kaselezo* (Breakwater, 1985), which in their own way criticize the alienating nature of the Haitian political structure. *Kaselezo* is particularly interesting because it is a one-act play about the oppression of women, developed by the author along with his troupe of actors. In this work, traditions of carnival masks and vaudou ritual combine with the interactive aesthetic of *spiralisme* to produce a stinging attack on misogyny and the patriarchal nature of Haitian society. His best-known work, however, is the play *Pelin-Tet* (Head traps), which deals with the experience of exile. The success of this work is ironic, since Etienne himself has never been in exile. This play is built around the dialogue between two Haitian characters living in a basement apartment in New York. One is an intellectual and the other a worker. The exchange between them deals not only with the difficulties of exile but the social and economic disparities that separate the haves and have-nots, the educated and the uneducated in Haitian society. This play has been successful both inside and outside Haiti.

It is an exaggeration to suggest that all writing within Haiti is done in Creole. However, literature from within Haiti cannot avoid the emergence of Creole along with the masses in the Lavalas movement. The use of Creole has also changed; it no longer needs to be a political statement in itself for younger writers but has, like any other language, to be transformed aesthetically for literary purposes. Younger writers in Haiti are generally more relaxed about the Creole issue. For instance, a writer like Lyonel Trouillot, who has been living in Haiti since 1982, writes in both French and Creole about the teeming and convulsive nature of contemporary Haitian society. In a similar way, Gary Victor also addresses the everyday concerns of contemporary Haitian politics and society. His best-known work is a series of humorous pieces that was published in the local press and collected in a book entitled *Albert Buron ou profil d'une élite* (Albert Buron, or an elite's profile, 1988). This irreverent, satirical chronicle of everyday life in Haiti is both informative in itself and particularly geared to a local public. The texts are arranged as a series of "audiences," or storytelling sessions, which hark back to similar experiments done in the past to bring together oral and literary modes of narration.

In a recent assessment of Caribbean literature written in French, one critic has proposed that there might be as many as three different literatures that need to be taken into account: an international literature with a foreign readership; a national literature that suffers from few readers and political upheaval, and a literature in Creole that survives in performance and in the local media.[3] Haiti does fit generally into the critic's description, and perhaps these categories are extended to include writing by Haitians in English in the United States. Haitian literature and culture are now at an important juncture. No one is sure how these various literary constituencies and their implications for a homogeneous national culture will evolve in the future. One thing seems certain. Even if there are divisions on the intellectual and literary levels between the various Haitian communities, the performing arts, particularly theatre and music, may have emerged as a crucial bond not only between literate and illiterate in Haiti but between Haitians on the outside and those on the inside.

NOTES

1. Jean-Paul Sartre, "Orphée noir," in *Anthologie de la nouvelle poésie nègre et malgache de langue française*, ed. L. S. Senghor (Paris: Presses Universitaires de France, 1948), xv.

2. Rene Depestre, "La revolution de 1946 est pour demain," in *1946–1976 Trente ans de pouvoir Noir en Haiti* (Lasalle: Collectif Paroles, 1976), 28.

3. Ulrich Fleischmann, "The Formation of a Literary Discourse: One, Two or Three Literatures," in *A History of Literature in the Caribbean: Vol. 1, Hispanic and Francophone Regions*, ed. A. James Arnold (Amsterdam: John Benjamins, 1994), 319.

7

The Performing Arts

IT IS COMMONPLACE to observe that the Caribbean is famous for its music. The twentieth century saw the international acceptance of Caribbean musical styles that range from Puerto Rican salsa to calypso from Trinidad, from French Caribbean *zouk* to Jamaican reggae. However, few countries in the Caribbean can provide the variety of musical rhythms and dance styles found in Haiti. This is largely so because of the plural nature of Haitian society. Haiti's agrarian, peasant population has provided musicologists and anthropologists with rich material for research on musical forms that accompany worship, work, and Carnival. On the other hand, Haiti's urban culture has provided a range of musical styles that takes us from the classical *meringue* in the nineteenth century to the contemporary innovations of *ra ra* rock, a mixture of high-tech rock with traditional, ritual rhythms. As is the case with other art forms, such as literature and painting, peasant culture has infiltrated urban Haitian music and is invariably the ultimate test for the authenticity of national musical expression.

It was also especially true in the twentieth century that various ideological movements made Haitian peasant culture, particularly peasant religion, important in the arts as a whole. The new cultural respectability with which peasant culture had been endowed since the 1920s extended to music and dance. Interest in folk forms and the performing arts was often encouraged by foreign visitors during and after the U.S. occupation. In the 1940s in particular, along with the discovery of primitive art by American investors, Katherine Dunham reinvigorated dance forms in the United States by drawing on possession rituals and dance ceremonies that she had observed in Haiti during her stay there in 1938. She was followed by Lavinia Williams, who popularized Haitian dance outside Haiti and frequently toured with the drummer Ti ro-ro, who had achieved an international reputation as a concert drummer. Interest in Haiti folk forms in the United States does in fact predate the visits of people like Dunham and Williams. In the nineteenth century, the New Orleans composer and pianist Louis Moreau Gottschalk, who had Haitian links, was one of the first in the United States to take Haitian music and dance seriously in his compositions. He was followed by another composer from Louisiana, Henri Fourrier, who used Haitian rhythms and themes in his work. Indeed, a number of musical and folk influences from Haiti are apparent in Louisiana's songs and dances.

Musical ethnography was the reason given for a trip to Haiti in 1928 by African American composer Clarence Cameron White and librettist John Frederick Matheus in search of musical materials for an opera. The opera, entitled *Ouanga!*, dealt with the Haitian revolution and was first performed in 1932 in Chicago and later in the 1950s at the Metropolitan Opera and Carnegie Hall in New York City. In the 1950s the African American opera star Marian Anderson performed in Haiti along with a folkloric choir. It is not coincidental that Matheus, White, Williams, and Dunham were African Americans, for the idea of forging links across the black diaspora through musical ethnography was fashionable in United States in the 1920s and 1930s. The presence of the artist William Scott in Port-au-Prince, as we have seen, can be viewed as another example of this kind of cultural tourism.

Despite the recognition abroad and the interest in Haitian folk forms in the United States, Haitian popular music was frowned on for a long time by the country's elite and remained unavailable on record until foreign ethnographers saw the importance of the music and dance in the peasantry. One of the difficulties that plagued Haitian music in the early stages was the lack of interest or investment in recording technology. Haiti lagged behind the rest of the Caribbean in this regard. The first recordings of traditional Haitian music were made by Harold Courlander in the 1930s in his *Songs and Dances of Haiti*. Since then there have been recorded arrangements of folk songs for choir by Michele Déjean, Martha Jean-Claude, and Emérante de Pradines. Later, with the widespread use of magnetic tape and the intensifying links with the United States, Haitian music became more available within Haiti and throughout North America in the 1950s. Indeed, the existence of external facilities and markets has much to do with the survival of Haitian musicians. This is especially true today, since a large Haitian diaspora and the label "world music" allow for a wide circulation of Haitian material. As with the visual arts, international acceptance has become vital to success in Haitian music.

Music has played a key role in the social and political developments in Haiti, especially in the twentieth century. The increasing influence of radio and recorded music in a country that is massively illiterate is part of the explanation for the prominence of music in social mobilization. The importance of music in Haitian culture as a whole is also significant. Music is not just entertainment. This is evident in the way that political regimes in Haiti have attempted to appropriate music and mass rituals like Carnival in order to maintain control or popularity and also in the way that political protest is expressed through music. The use of popular music and the manipulation of Carnival under the Duvaliers is a clear example of the need to mobilize the masses through music in order to promote the state's interests. In more recent times, music has become the driving force behind former President Aristide's Lavalas movement, which derived its very name from a popular song. Aristide has composed songs that promote his political ideas. The role of the *ra ra* rock group Boukman Eksperyans in the electoral victory of the Lavalas movement is also important. It could also be argued that the enormously popular hit by this group, entitled "Calfou Dangere" (Dangerous Crossroads), which was banned by the Haitian military, was instrumental in keeping alive the opposition movement that eventually restored Aristide to power. This example is just another dramatic illustration of the capacity of music in Haiti to empower the masses.

FOLK FORMS

The musical legacy of the elite in the nineteenth century in Haiti was the classical *meringue*. The term *meringue* in Haiti is decidedly ambiguous. It can refer to any music that is popular in origin as well as a kind of graceful concert music. Since the late nineteenth century, the effort to create an original Haitian music has led to efforts to incorporate folk elements into classical forms in order to produce a national music. Anton Jaegerhuber was an early-twentieth-century Haitian composer of classical music that was strongly influenced by folk melodies and rhythms. Haitian composers such as Occide Jeanty and Ludovic Lamothe were the best-known exponents of the art of the classical *meringue*. The turn of the twentieth century in Haiti also provided the wonderfully nostalgic song by Othello Bayard, "Haiti Cherie" (Dear Haiti), which has come to epitomize Haitian patriotism. However, production of folk-influenced art music is modest and often completely omitted from accounts of Haitian culture. In general, the musical legacy of the nineteenth century is poor compared to the literature written in that century. The francophile elite as a whole had little time for an indigenous music and used as musical accompaniment a string orchestra whose repertoire was a very European mix of polkas, waltzes, and quadrilles. The local *meringues* were the only departure from this largely European fare.

On the other hand, the peasant on his small plot of land deep in the mountains produced a music that was closely associated with his religious beliefs. Because of the pervasive influence of the vaudou religion and the importance of music and dance to that religion, most aspects of peasant culture are related to vaudou rituals. The music of agrarian practices, Carnival, and other forms of entertainment is to a greater or lesser extent colored by vaudou. The sacred rattles of the *houngan*, the a capella singing of the *hounsis*, the blowing of the *lambi*, or conch shell, and, very important, the drumming are essential features of any vaudou ceremony. The other instrument of importance in Haiti is the enormous bamboo base-flute, or *vaccine*, which is about four feet long. Its repetitive one note is used to accompany the singing in *ra ra* bands during Lent. However, it is the drum in its various manifestations that dominates musical instruments in Haiti; it can range from the flat drum used in communal work brigades to the giant *assotor* that has now disappeared from vaudou ceremonies.

Much emphasis has justifiably been put on drumming, and the drum is considered a sacred object that can bring on possession through its rhythmic insistence. The drummers are never possessed but control the ceremony, fusing the worshipers into a single rhythmic whole. An ethnologist who took particular interest in drumming in vaudou vividly described the powerful influence of the drum on the possessed individual after her 1947 visit to Haiti:

> [T]he defenseless person is buffeted by each great stroke, as the drummer sets out to 'beat the loa into his head'. The person cringes with each large beat, as if the drum mallet descended on his very skull; he ricochets about the peristyle, clutching blindly at the arms, which are extended to support him, pirouettes wildly on one leg, recaptures balance for a brief moment, only to be hurtled forward again by another great blow from the drum.[1]

Besides the power of percussion, the singing of the vaudou chorus is vital to the invocation of the *loa*s, since it represents a way of preserving the religious memory of the community and also expresses the devotion of the worshipers. Since nothing in the vaudou religion is written down, singing, which is handed down from generation to generation, is a way of preserving tradition. The singing, which is performed by the priest's female chorus of *hounsis*, is a clear example of African retentions in Haitian folk culture. The songs tend to be chants whose emotional effect is heightened by repetition and countless modulations of the melodic line. The rhythmic structure of this singing as well as the very posture of the singers is identifiably African.

The songs of vaudou are dedicated to each specific *loa* and grouped into the categories of the various *nanchons*. These are distinct from songs that are used for secular activities such as the *coumbite*, or collective labor ritual, the *ra ra* processions during the season of Lent, and ordinary parties of *bamboches*. The song is initiated by the choirmaster, or *hungenikon*, who launches it by stridently intoning the first lines, which are then picked up by the *hounsi* choir. The songs are short invocations to the deities and belong to a traditional repertoire. There is no injunction against adding references to a contemporary incident, and sometimes these improvisations can give birth to new songs, thereby extending the repertoire. These new creations can then be spread because of the prestige of a particular *hounfor* or because of the musical merit of the composition.

Another interesting feature of these songs is the ambiguity of the language, which can be both the voice of the *loa*s as well as the expression of the sentiments of the worshipers. The actual meaning of the words is not easy to decipher; they are often sung in a "language" made up of words from African languages handed down over time. These songs can also contain moral judgment in the form of a proverb and are sometimes used to point to actual situations or quarrels. These *chants point* can emerge from a particular situation and are then memorized so as to enter the liturgy. This is also true of secular singing, where songs are related to incidents in a community and then repeated during communal work or a *ra ra* procession. In this regard, the role the troubadour, or popular singer in Haiti, who is expected to comment on everyday life in his versions of the *chants point*, is related to the figure of the vaudou choirmaster, or *hungenikon*, and the *simidor*, or leader of the *coumbite* (work) brigade.

Vaudou is not only a sung religion but also a danced religion. Dancing is prominent in all ceremonies because it is seen as a vital link with the supernatural. When a dancer is possessed, he or she can be spurred into a series of spectacular improvisations that are interpreted as examples of the grace and suppleness of the *loa*. The dancing in Haitian popular culture has often led to stereotypes of "orgiastic" and "chaotic," because no clear distinction is made between sacred and profane, nor are the distinctions between solemn and sexual rigidly enforced. In general, no one dances with a partner, and the emphasis on bodily self-expression leads to the physically uninhibited nature of the dance in Haitian culture. The lack of inhibition also very often leads to displays of sexual suggestiveness, which nevertheless rigidly avoid body contact. The *banda* dance dedicated to the *guedes* is the most explicitly sexual of the popular dances.

In a vaudou ceremony the dancers, who are also singing, revolve counter-clockwise around the central pole, or *poteau-mitan* of the temple, moving to the beat of the drums. The shoulders and the hips are more active than the feet in these dances. Occasionally, at the signal given by the drum, there is a break or an off-beat in the rhythm, and an individual dancer can break from the general flow in order to improvise. These breaks can throw individual participants into a state of frenzy that precedes possession. While dancing, the women grasp the hem of their dresses with both hands and lower it in time with the music. The men dance with their hands holding the ends of a cloth they often wear around their necks.

In the same way that each vaudou *nanchon* has its own drums and songs, so it also has its own dances. Therefore, there are *petro* dances as well as *rada* dances, of which the best known is the *yanvalou*. This dance is performed with the body leaning forward, knees bent, with undulations that spread from the shoulders down the back. The undulating movement suggests the waves of the sea or of the movements of a snake, and the dance can be dedicated either to Agoué, the sea god, or Damballah, the snake god. The dancers move not forward but sideways, by sliding their feet in this direction following the beat of the drum. Dances to the other *loa*s, such as the *nago* in honor of Ogun (the god of fire and war), can be more rapid and violent. In the *petro* dances the feet may play a more important role, with the dancer stretching one hand in front while resting the other on one hip.

The conscious use of folk forms to create a national musical style was undertaken in the late 1930s. This phenomenon should be seen in the context of the need to promote a sanitized version of Haitian peasant culture abroad. The mulatto status quo had less difficulty with folkloric choirs and dances than they had with the promotion of vaudou by Haiti's nationalist radicals. The same president who could sanction the Catholic Church's anti-superstitious campaign was able to support folk music and art. This promotion of folklore intensified during the presidency of Estimé. The international exposition of 1949 was planned as a showcase for Haitian culture, and the performing arts were to be highlighted. The influence of visitors to Haiti like Katherine Dunham and Lavinia Williams had not only made

Haitian folkloric dance popular abroad but had encouraged locally the formation of dance troupes that used a national choreography based on vaudou dance. Stylization and a desire to make the dance less "vulgar" for the tourist trade often led to banality and a sanitization of folk forms. However, there have been worthy efforts to create a national repertoire from folk music and dance in the postwar years.

For instance, Haiti's first folklore troupe was established in 1941 by Jean Léon Destiné, who had previously danced with Dunham. He went on to direct the more professional Troupe Nationale Folklorique in the 1950s by recruiting dancers from all over Haiti. He was the first to use the drummer Ti ro-ro in his national dance theatre. This troupe and the one later organized by the singer Emérante de Pradines performed regularly at the newly constructed, open-air Theatre de Verdure, which was also a venue for a number of folk choirs. This period represented a moment of legendary creativity in the use of folk material in Haitian music. In 1949, the song "Panama m' tonbe" was established as part of a national repertoire, and singers such as Lumane Casimir and Martha Jean Claude emerged and became models for folk singers to come. Just like the visual arts, Haitian music and dance benefited from the postwar boom and the increase in tourism in the northern Caribbean. This trend would continue in the 1950s, when Port-au-Prince became increasingly popular as a tourist playground and nightlife flourished under President Magloire. It ceased only when the Duvalierist dictatorship turned ugly in the 1960s.

POPULAR MUSIC

The relationship between folk forms and other kinds of music can best be explained in terms of the need to incorporate peasant or working-class musical expression into a form that would be recognizably national. There is therefore a constant reaching down into folk forms for stylistic devises, rhythmic patterns, or melodic ideas in order to turn these forms into something more acceptable in a class or national context. Traditional forms become the basis for a kind of resistance through indigenization. This phenomenon is as true of the classical composers of the Haitian *meringue* of the nineteenth century as it is of the need to politicize through folk roots in contemporary musical expression. In the same way that music reaches downward in order to establish its authenticity, it is also influenced by contact with the outside world. This is, of course, no different from the literary Indigenous movement, which was influenced by the European avant-grade in its championing of local culture. Romantic nationalism in art music is as responsible for the creation of the classical *meringue* in the nineteenth century as American jazz was in influencing Haitian music after the U.S. occupation.

The occupation had a disruptive effect on Haitian culture at all levels. This is as true of music as of other areas of cultural expression. The arrival of U.S. troops and the exposure of Haitians to North American culture meant the end of European cultural influence in the elite and the emergence of a middle class whose tastes would be shaped by the U.S. presence. The elite tried to cling to their francophile attitudes as a way of resisting what they saw as the barbaric, Anglo-Saxon presence of the North Americans. For instance, they objected to the tax imposed on grand pianos and saw the fact that the United States did not favor the teaching of the classics in schools as an affront to Haitian nationalism. However, U.S. control of the northern Caribbean in the first decade of the twentieth century meant the end of European influence. In Haiti it meant a new cultural orientation, more focused on the United States and the Caribbean.

As far as music was concerned, the occupation meant the end of the string orchestra, with its European repertoire, and the decline in popularity of the Haitian *meringue*. Haiti was exposed from the 1920s onward to two of the most important forces that shaped modern Haitian music: the African American jazz bands of the time and Cuban music. The influence of the African American jazz band was so pervasive in the 1920s that the word *jazz* came to mean "dance band" in Haiti. The enthusiasm for jazz was also reinforced by the negrophile interest in African American culture that was in vogue in Paris in the 1920s. In Haiti, jazz bands played at the exclusive clubs of the elite as well as at the brothels filled with Dominican prostitutes that were frequented by U.S. soldiers. Since U.S. imperialism in the northern Caribbean had also led to the political control of Cuba, there was increased contact with Cuban culture and music in particular. This contact existed at all levels, from migrant sugar workers from Haiti to tourists from the elite. By the end of the occupation, Cuban-style dance music, or troubadour music, had replaced the earlier jazz influence, giving a definitive Latin American stamp to modern Haitian music.

Cuban musical styles such as the *son*, rumba, *bolero*, and the *guaracha* penetrated Haiti, quickly merging at times with the traditional *meringue*. Haiti's musical evolution would henceforth be profoundly shaped by Cuban music, which was combined with a local repertory. By the 1940s Cuban orchestras, especially Sonora Matancera, visited Haiti regularly and performed on weekends at the nightclubs and hotels that had sprung up in Pétionville. Cuban-style music threatened to eclipse all forms of local music. "The reign of Cuban music in Port-au-Prince was so complete that the publication *Haiti Journal* felt it necessary to launch a campaign in favor of the Meringue in 1945 and to inaugurate a meringue competition."[2]

The postwar years in Haiti bear witness to a convergence of two distinct musical traditions that emerged from the U.S. occupation. On the one hand the occupation led to the musical penetration of Haiti by foreign music— in particular African American jazz, but more important, Cuban dance bands. On the other hand, a nationalistic movement was championing local folklore and the vaudou religion in particular as the basis for a national culture. These two trends, one pointing outside to a Latin American orientation for Haitian music, the other inward-turning and folk-oriented, dominate the next two decades of Haitian music.

The impact of cultural nationalism on Haitian music can be seen in the creation of a musical style called vaudou-jazz, which was popularized by a band of middle-class musicians in the 1940s called the Jazz des Jeunes. The strength and popularity of this band was related to its ability to fashion dance music from indigenous musical forms. These musicians responded to the call for indigenization by adapting big band arrangements to local vaudou rhythms and *ra ra* songs. Their urban neotraditionalist music also at times criticized the traditional mulatto elite for its preference for foreign styles and its scorn for anything local. Ideologically this group was deeply influenced by the cult of authenticity and the afrocentric orientation of the noiriste movement. However, in order to achieve commercial success, this meant a shrewd mix of popular cosmopolitan musical styles with indigenous rhythms. It was at this time that the singer Guy Durosier rose to fame with a rival dance band, L'Orchestre Saieh, which also specialized in a more polished form of vaudou-jazz. When a black middle-class schoolteacher, Dumarsais Estimé, was elected president in 1946, this event was almost seen as the vindication of vaudou-jazz. These groups would also appear regularly at the Theatre de Verdure along with other folkloric acts. Vaudou-jazz continued to be popular into the 1950s and paved the way musically for the success of noiriste politics in 1957.

While the Bicentenary Exposition of 1949 promoted folkloric vaudou-jazz, the nightclubs of Pétionville featured a cosmopolitan mix of big-band jazz and Latin dance numbers. This was the highpoint of nightlife for modern Haiti. It would all come to an abrupt end in the social strife that preceded the election of 1957 and the aggressive thuggery that accompanied the early years of Duvalierism. Race-infused politics also meant the state appropriation of all cultural activity, and this extended to vaudou-jazz. This music lost both its novelty and its creative edge in the early Duvalier years. The new urban groups were more interested in partying to the music of Nemours Jean-

Baptiste, whose new beat—*compas direct*, as it was called—was far more attractive than the wholesome, state-approved music of the Jazz des Jeunes.

The music called *compas* was commercially created from the Dominican *meringue*, which had become enormously popular in Haiti in the 1950s and eclipsed the earlier influence of Cuban music. Dance bands now came to Haiti from the Dominican Republic instead of Havana. The *meringue*, which was heavily promoted by Dominican nationalism, also reached Haiti through Dominican radio stations and was the music of choice in Haitian brothels, which were stocked with women from the Dominican Republic. Taking advantage of this lively new beat, the Haitian musician Nemours Jean-Baptiste created a Haitian version of the Dominican *meringue* that he called "*compas direct*." This music and the dance that went along with it were linked to commercial success and had little to do with celebrating Haiti's folkloric past. *Compas* marks the emergence of a music industry in Haiti and is the first Haitian popular music to achieve commercial success.

Nemours used his band to give all sections of Haitian society access to his new beat, from the elegant soirees held by the elite in Pétionville to the rural dances that took place in the country parts. His music was also popularized through weekly broadcasts on Radio Haiti. Success meant commercial sponsorship and ultimately access to an international market. It also meant rivalry. *Compas* spawned other related beats in the 1960s that were part of the musical rivalry that dominated commercial music in the early Duvalier years. One of Nemours' saxophonists, Weber Sicot, created his own variation of the *compas* that he called *cadence rempart*. Commercial changes in Haiti's musical culture and the emergence of a mass audience are apparent in the Carnivals of this period, where rival bands each had their own sponsors and amplified sound systems. This kind of commercial rivalry in the field of entertainment was the only sign of competing groups in a Haiti totally monopolized by Duvalierist politics. This would not remain the case for long; Duvalierist sponsorship soon became important to both bands, as the state used every means at its disposal to spread its ideology and the cult of Duvalier.

In the 1960s the rise of rock music internationally also registered in Haiti and marked another shift in commercial popular music. This interest in foreign music among the children of the middle class was frowned on by the hardline Duvalierists, who at that time were aggressively antagonistic to U.S. foreign policy. *Compas* was therefore modified to suit a new format. The big band was replaced by the combo or mini-jazz. The resulting effect of this new format of two guitars, a saxophone, a bass, and drums created a new version of *Compas* that was purely recreational and geared to a teenage audience. Despite the inauspicious beginnings of this music—many of the youthful musicians were untrained, and Duvalierism was at its most ruth-less—these combos proliferated and invaded other islands like Martinique and Guadeloupe in the 1970s, eventually spreading to Haiti's communities in exile by the end of the decade. Some of the popular mini-jazz groups were lbo Combo, Les Shleu Shleu, Skah Shah, Les Fréres Dejean, and Tabou Combo. Their cheerful sound marks a strong contrast to the dark days of Duvalierism of the late 1960s. Lyrics never mattered to these groups; they made no attempt to react to Haiti's social reality, which was steadily wors-ening both economically and ecologically.

The 1970s meant a more relaxed political climate under Jean Claude Du-valier, who was a supporter of the mini-jazz movement. Liberalization brought foreign investment and factory building to the capital. It meant more wealth among members of the middle class and the supporters of the regime, and also signified increasing hardship in the countryside. The *compas* of the mini-jazz groups avoided any comment on social reality. It was escapist en-tertainment and suited the regime perfectly. Opportunities were nevertheless limited for local musicians, and state patronage was important to survival. The lure of Haiti's diaspora in New York had also intensified, and by the mid-1970s the mini-jazz groups began to establish themselves in North American cities like Miami and New York, where there were high concen-trations of Haitians. It is in these exile communities that the domination of Haitian music by *compas* would be challenged as a greater social engagement was called for with the weakening of Duvalierism in the mid-1980s.

Compas did attempt to respond to the need for greater political engage-ment in the music of the charismatic singer Ti-Manno. He had been shaped by the politics of the Haitian diaspora in North America and wrote lyrics critical of social injustice in Haiti. He also introduced elements of Jamaican reggae to *compas* as well as diverse musical styles from salsa to Dominican *cadence*. Ti-Manno's music meant a breakthrough for *compas* in both estab-lishing the music's international credentials as well as giving what was essen-tially frivolous dance music a progressive political thrust. The *angaje*, or politically committed dimension to his music, was intensified with the re-cordings done with the band Gemini Express. He never abandoned the el-ement of pleasure in *compas* but was unique in adding an element of protest that made his music unique at the time. He died before Duvalier fell from power, but his example did have some effect on *compas* by encouraging other musicians to become more politically aware in their lyrics.

Developments in Haitian music in the 1980s took place almost exclusively outside the country. There was a revival of interest in Haitian folk forms, especially vaudou and *ra ra* musical traditions. The exile communities were freer to experiment with musical styles, which were now being combined with leftist politics and anti-Duvalierist sentiment. The *mizik rasin*, or roots music, movement that emerged in the Haitian diaspora was different from the vaudou-jazz of the 1950s. It was not merely a matter of creating a dance music with a stylistic authenticity. Roots music was a strategy to bring a new spiritual respectability to a religion that had been manipulated by the state in order to oppress Haitians more effectively. It was also influenced by the message of spiritual solidarity in the Rastafarian movement on the neighboring island of Jamaica. What reggae superstar Bob Marley had done for Jamaica and the black diaspora, *mizik razin* was expected to do for Haiti and the Haitian diaspora. It was a strategy that had a ready international market, that required explicit authenticity in music to be sold in the "world music" format. This new orientation for vaudou-based popular music, or *vaudou ajaye*, from Haiti has been explained in the following way:

> The mizik razin bands didn't see their work as folklore or as something conceptually distinct from Vodou-as-religion, but as an extension of Voudou spirituality into other realms. Boukman Eksperyans labeled their music "Voudou adjaye" a term used for the dances at a peristil (temple) that follow ceremonies. Trance plays a critical role in authentic roots music performances.[3]

This new militant orientation in Haitian music was apparent in the late 1970s with the formation of Magnum Band in Miami in 1976, which dealt explicitly with the fate of the Haitian people, and the recordings of the singer Toto Bissainthe, who was inspired by vaudou songs. Atis Endepandan, Soley Leve, Ayizan, and Troupe Kwidor in New York were just a few of the groups that pioneered a protest, or *angaje*, music based on vaudou rhythms and indigenous instruments. By 1980 *compas* was twenty-five years old, and a new politicized music had begun to lead the anti-Duvalier opposition. In Haiti, the peasantry was being increasingly politicized by the teachings of the Ti Legliz, creating a mass audience within Haiti for a militant populist music.

It is within this context that we must consider the importance of the singer and songwriter Manno Charlemagne. Charlemagne, who was raised among Haiti's poor, had a firsthand experience of injustice and misery. He rose to prominence in the 1970s with his *angaje* songs, which began to attract attention in Haiti. A gifted lyricist, Charlemagne's Creole songs were never about entertainment. They were cleverly composed both to reflect the harsh lives of the poor and to not refer directly to the Duvalier regime. This would not go on for too long, and in 1980 Duvalier began a rigid crackdown on dissident movements. Charlemagne left Haiti clandestinely that year. The albums of Creole protest music he released in the early 1980s in the United States established his reputation as a major figure in the anti-Duvalier opposition and more generally a critic of international imperialism.

Charlemagne returned to Haiti after Duvalier fell in 1986 and immediately became active in the *dechoukaj* movement. While he, like many of the protest groups, saw *compas* as politically compromised escapist music, he did not share the belief in vaudou that was becoming common among practitioners of *mizik razin*. He was much more interested in the revolutionary potential of popular music than in vaudou theology. During the coup that drove President Aristide into exile, Charlemagne attempted to mobilize support for Aristide. He was arrested and on his release sought asylum in the Argentine embassy. Under pressure from a campaign by celebrities in the United States led by the filmmaker Jonathan Demme, Charlemagne was allowed out of the country. After democracy was restored in 1994, he was elected mayor of Port-au-Prince.

Mizik razin makes it full-blown appearance with the formation of the group Boukman Eksperyans in 1978. This group took the name of the priest who officiated at the Bois Caiman ceremony that launched the Haitian revolution. They therefore promoted, along with their anti-Duvalier politics, a vision of vaudou as a symbol of both a Haitian and a pan-African identity. They were interested not only in political resistance but in the idea that vaudou might represent a source of spiritual regeneration, a spiritual solution to the psychic predicament of both the Haitian masses and the Haitian diaspora. In this regard they followed closely the attitude to religion in the Rastafarian movement. Beyond the idea of spiritual and ethnic unification, the members of Boukman Eksperyans experimented with styles and rhythms drawn from vaudou and mixed with other international black musical forms. With the fall of Duvalierism, *mizik razin* literally took center stage in Haiti.

The fall of Duvalierism was seen by musicians within Haiti as an opportunity for musical *dechoukaj*. *Mizik razin* became the more extreme manifestation of the pro-Lavalas political orientation of other musical experiments that used vaudou and *ra ra* rhythms. The musicians from within Haiti who participated in this movement were called simply *nouvel generasyon*, or "new generation." With the advent of elections in 1990 and Aristide's candidacy, the roots music phenomenon became fully involved in local politics. This marks a big change from the Duvalier years, when popular music was condemned to blandness. Carnival in 1991, after Aristide's victory, was dominated by the *angaje* music of this new roots-oriented *ra ra* and vaudou music. The importance of Boukman Eksperyans and a local roots band called Ram grew during the repression after the military coup that ousted Aristide.

In 1992 Boukman Eksperyans was nominated for a Grammy award because of the success of their album *Vaudou adjae*. This feat had never been achieved before by a Haitian band. International success may have protected them from violent attacks during the military coup. However, their song "Calfou Dangere" (Dangerous Crossroads) became the rallying cry of anti-army protest during Aristide's three years of exile. This song, with its imagery of spiritual resistance drawn from vaudou and the symbol of the crossroads as the point of reckoning between oppressors and oppressed, became so popular that it was banned from Carnival in 1992 and not played on national television. A concert attended by more than 1,000 young people was broken up by teargas before "Calfou Dangere" could be performed. As a *New York Times* music reporter wrote, "in only three days 'Calfou Dangere' became a hit from Port-au-Prince to Flatbush, Brooklyn. It also became an anthem for supporters of the democratically elected President, the Rev. Jean-Bertrand Aristide."[4]

The roots band Ram, which combined high-tech rock with traditional Haitian rhythms, was led by Richard Morse, the son of the folk singer Emérante de Pradines. After Aristide's ouster they released a new version of the song "Fey," which had been sung decades earlier by Morse's mother. This song, which warns the listener not to forget someone who is absent, was immediately interpreted by the Haitian people as a comment on the tense political situation in Haiti. Ram followed this hit with a *ra ra* song entitled "Anbago" for the 1992 Carnival. This time the politics of the song were more direct, especially when performed before a huge crowd on the Champs de Mars. Ram, like Boukman Eksperyans, had found a way to use vaudou-derived dance music as a catalyst for communicating with a mass audience. Once more politics had projected protest music to the forefront of the resistance movement.

Given the turbulence of the last decade, the years of military repression and the worsening state of the economy, Haiti would seem to be the last place one would expect to find a vibrant popular music. Quite the opposite has occurred, as a new burst of creativity has greeted the end of dictatorship in Haiti. A revival of interest in both political radicalism and peasant culture has propelled Haitian music into becoming the most vibrant aspect of modern Haitian culture. In a politically and economically divided society, music has become a way of bridging the gap in Haiti between town and country, between mass-based political movements and the younger generation from comfortable neighborhoods. Music has also been the bond between the Haitian diaspora and Haitians at home. Current music trends indicate the connections that have emerged between Haitian popular music and the mainstream of American popular music. Haitian musicians have no difficulty wearing dreadlocks (a hairstyle formed by matting or braiding) and using Jamaican reggae or even Jamaican rap music or dance hall in their compositions. Even *compas* has had a new lease on life because of the new creative surge. Always popular with Haitian dancers, this music, which once avoided political themes, now has a new bite. It too forms part of the new sophisticated blend of musical styles and eloquent political commentary that characterizes Haitian music at the beginning of the twenty-first century.

The spread of modern Haitian music, its success as an instrument of popular resistance, and its ability to forge links between Haiti and the rest of the world would not be possible without the mass media. If the protest song by Boukman Eksperyans, "Calfou Dangere," was a hit within three days of its release, it was because it could be recorded from radio broadcasts and then immediately replayed and copied for a mass audience. Haitian music has come a long way since the early recordings made by the German radio station owner Ricardo Widmaier in the late 1930s and the live broadcast of concerts of vaudou-jazz in the 1950s. The path broken by *compas* in establishing itself as a fully commercial music using modern recording technology has been followed by more recent musical forms that politicized the content of the music. Whether it is roots music, *ra ra* rock, or the *compas* revival, Haitian music is now an integral part of mass politics in Haiti and big business. Record shops located in Haitian neighborhoods all over the United States and Canada serve as distribution centers and also produce much of the new music. Their market is no longer just within Haiti and the diaspora. The United States itself, because of the widespread interest in world music, now provides a market, as do the French Overseas Departments of Martinique, Guadeloupe, and Guyane in the Caribbean.

NOTES

1. Maya Deren, *The Voodoo Gods* (London: Thames and Hudson, 1953), 228.

2. Gage Averill, *A Day for the Hunter, A Day for the Prey: Popular Music and Power in Haiti* (Chicago: University of Chicago Press, 1997), 54.

3. Averill, *A Day for the Hunter*, 140.

4. Daisann McLane, "The Haitian Beat Thrives in Times of Suffering," *The New York Times*, March 8, 1992.

8

The Visual Arts and Architecture

ONE OF THE MOST surprising features of Haitian society is the contrast between the ravages of misery and misrule on the outside and the rich, imaginative inner world of the ordinary Haitian. As has been written in an influential book, *The Drum and the Hoe: Life and Lore of the Haitian People*, the Haitian is "outwardly simple and poor, but inwardly he is a complicated and rich man."[1] The dusty streets of the capital, Port-au-Prince, for instance, are polluted and overcrowded, the buildings ramshackle. Yet painting almost seems to be a kind of second language, judging by the brightly decorated buses or "tap taps," the political murals and artistic graffiti on the city's walls. The bustling central iron market of the capital is filled with arts and crafts stalls. There is also the boulevard, near the port, where hundred of paintings can be bartered for daily.

The paradox of this amazing and prolific creativity in the face of sterile and brutal economic and political realities distinguishes Haiti from the rest of the Caribbean. The richness of Haitian popular culture and the interest in painting and carving is unequalled elsewhere in the region. For the longest while, this art was overlooked by a supercilious society with its parochial and Eurocentric elite, which was far more interested in artistic fashions abroad than in the decorative arts of an illiterate peasantry, especially since popular art forms were closely related to the practice of vaudou. This creativity did not present itself as art, however, but could be found in the most banal places: on paper kites, calabashes (ground-shell utensils), bottles, vaudou altars, Carnival masks, and baskets. As one art critic put it, "the peasant has been content to dance over his finest drawings,"[2] in reference to the ephemeral *veves* traced on the peristyle floor to invoke the deities. Recognition came, however, in the 1940s with the emergence of an art market in Haiti. This phenomenon, which is not much more than fifty years old, is as much the product of the nationalist plea for the recognition of the value of popular culture as it was the discovery of Haitian painters by sympathetic foreigners.

In the 1940s Haitian art erupted onto the international art scene. Its sudden and spectacular emergence is usually attributed to the U.S. watercolorist DeWitt Peters. The Centre d'Art was established as a joint Haitian-American venture in 1944 by Peters, who had come to Haiti as an English teacher; it was a key factor in the discovery and marketing of Haitian art. The visit in the following year by French surrealist André Breton, who claimed Haiti's popular artists as true surrealists in his book *Surrealism and Painting* (1947), established the credentials of Haiti's self-taught artists. Pierre Mabille, Jean-Paul Sartre, and Alejo Carpentier were just a few of the intellectuals who visited Haiti in the 1940s and praised the work of Haiti's primitive artists. An exhibition of paintings by the internationally respected Cuban painter Wifredo Lam at the same time at the Centre d'Art was instrumental in winning recognition for the center's activities. In the 1947 UNESCO exhibition in Paris, the work of the vaudou priest Hector Hippolyte dominated the show, which featured art from about fifty-five countries. From that time Haitian art has been closely associated with the vaudou religion and with the primitivist or Naive School of painters.

This discovery of Haitian art by the outside world put to rest an argument about the quality of popular Haitian art that had always bedeviled its acceptance. For a long time, Haitian textiles, paintings, and carvings were viewed as handicrafts rather than as fine art—essentially, as curiosities almost anonymously produced by mysterious cults, illiterate artists, and inscrutable beliefs. Today, any travel book on Haiti or the most ordinary tour guide has a major section on Haitian art and where it can be bought, clearly indicating the existence of an international market for Haitian popular art. Art may in some ways have led to the rehabilitation of the vaudou religion in the minds of foreigners. The very successful exhibition, entitled "The Sacred Arts of Haitian Vaudou," toured a number of major cities in the United States recently and demonstrated that the Haitian popular imagination is not simply obsessed with zombies and the supernatural.

The tastes of this international market have emphasized the folkloric nature of Haitian art. This labeling of all Haitian art has tended to obscure the complexities of the local art scene in Haiti. It not only led to the overproduction of so-called primitive works for the undiscriminating buyer but also created the distorted view that one need not look beyond the 1940s for the origins of Haitian art. Nothing could be further from the truth, but even an experienced anthropologist like Melville Herskovits lamented in his 1937 study, *Life in a Haitian Valley*, the absence of graphic and plastic arts in Haiti. There is certainly evidence of Haitian painting in the nineteenth century. Artistic activity was, for instance, encouraged by Henri Christophe, who established a school for Haitian painters. This art was meant to glorify the king and his court. There is also evidence of state-sponsored art activity during the presidencies of Soulouque and Geffrard, when academies of art were founded. There is less documentation of the arts of the peasantry before the twentieth century. Foreign commentators were unlikely to pursue art in the Haitian countryside. The elite were even less likely to consider the often ephemeral decorations associated with peasant rituals worthy of being called art.

The picture becomes much clearer during the U.S. occupation, when the artistic self-consciousness created among Haitians in 1928 led to a general renaissance. One Haitian ethnologist dismissed all previous attempts at art in Haiti with the sweeping statement, "Are a few sporadic demonstrations of painting and sculpture sufficient to characterize an artistic legacy?"[3] In the 1930s Pétion Savain (1906–1975), who deserves to be called the pioneer of modern Haitian art, took up Price-Mars' challenge. It seems that the U.S. occupation also fostered contact with visiting artists, which helped foster local art activity. In 1930, the visiting African American painter William Scott encouraged Savain and others to paint seriously. Scott was particularly interested in the peasantry and the countryside as artistic themes. The fact that Scott was black must have made him more acceptable at a time when anti-U.S. feeling was running high. Scott's interest in indigenous themes coupled with the strident call for a more authentic Haitian art by the radicals of *La Revue Indigene* became the catalysts for Savain's creativity.

Savain was close to some of the major literary figures of the time, such as Jacques Roumain, Philippe Thoby-Marcelin, and Normil Sylvain. He predictably attempted to apply indigenist precepts to the visual arts. He followed William Scott's lead and his early Haitian scenes, often painted in the manner of Le Douanier Rousseau or the French impressionists, found favor with such indigenist luminaries as Jacques Roumain and Philippe Thoby-Marcelin. The Indigenious movement prescribed a heavy dose of social reality for Haitian art, and Savain was therefore required to paint directly from observed reality. The blending of art and literature in an indigenist mode can be seen in Savain's novel on vaudou, *La case de Damballah* (Damballah's hut, 1939), which he illustrated with a series of woodcuts. Savain's tastes ultimately were drawn to brightly colored still life and to technical questions of volume and light. His painting entitled "Market" won a bronze medal in 1940 at the New York World's Fair. Subsequently, his best-known paintings were his geometrically stylized market scenes, with their crouching figures in semicircles and triangles. These have been copied to the point of becoming one of the unavoidable clichés of Haitian airport art.

Savain's work raised key questions of technique and authenticity within the framework of the populist politics of the Indigenous movement. His paintings were never spontaneous or intuitive but strove to appropriate modern styles in art in order to maintain a startling freshness and a calculated primitivism. A small group of artists, with similar concerns with evolving original forms and indigenous composition, formed around Savain. Painters such as George Ramponneau, Xavier Amiana, Antoine Derenoncourt, Raoul Dupoux, and Maurice Borno formed the Pont St. Geraud Group, named after the area in Port-au-Prince when they regularly met. Their work focused almost exclusively on Haitian scenes, quite often mixing idyllic images of the countryside with the seamier side of the city life. Technically their work was often precariously poised between a kind of mannered exoticism on the one hard and social realism on the other hand. This debate on what would constitute a Haitian aesthetic, which raged in literary circles at the time, would inevitably be reflected in the visual arts as well.

The 1930s were a very promising decade for Haitian art. Exhibitions and competitions were organized, and sponsorship was found for this new school of painters. Posts as professors of drawing were also funded in various schools by the state. The opening up of Haiti because of the occupation meant that artists, like their literary counterparts, could now travel more easily. Both Savain and Ramponneau traveled to the United States in the early 1940s to study art, and foreign artists also visited Haiti, especially from the United States. However, surviving economically in Haiti was a problem for artists. The elite was always uneasy with paintings that reproduced the harshness and squalor of Haitian social reality on canvas. Their unease turned to downright rejection in the 1940s, when the elite attempted to put distance between themselves and the emergent middle classes as well as the movement for cultural authenticity. In collusion with the Catholic Church, the elite waged a war on peasant culture through the anti-superstitious campaign. In so doing, as one observer explained, they shortsightedly destroyed valuable artifacts:

I was in Haiti in 1941 and I remember seeing in the back yards of presbyteries vast pyramids of drums, painted bowls, necklaces, talismans—all waiting for the day fixed for the joyous blaze which was to symbolize the victory of the Church over Satan.[4]

The question of how profoundly Haitian the work of these early pioneers was would be debated again and again, especially after the explosion of the self-taught painters in the 1940s onto the international art market. However, one cannot overlook the importance of these 1930s painters in preparing the way for a Haitian art to emerge. In a very practical sense, they would be among the first members of the Centre d'Art that Peters set up in 1944. Ramponneau and Borno were co-founders of the center, for instance, and Ramponneau its first treasurer. Even though the Centre d'Art became famous because of its promotion of Haiti's self-taught artists, some talented painters who could be seen as continuing the early work of Savain's group also exhibited at the center. Two clear examples of this sometimes overlooked phenomenon are Lucien Price and Luce Turnier. Price joined the Centre d'Art at its inception and was perhaps the first Haitian artist to move from figurative to abstract representation. Turnier joined the center a year later and also exhibited work that managed to successfully graft modernist styles onto Haitian themes. Both traveled to the United States and Europe, and both are examples of the creative use of modernism by Haitian painters.

HAITIAN PRIMITIVISM

The success of Haitian "primitives" in the 1940s has as much to do with the activities of Peters and his Centre d'Art as with the increasing acceptance of Caribbean art in general and Cuban art in particular in the United States and Europe.

[T]he Cuban vanguardia was the first Caribbean school to receive attention in Europe and North America. In 1944, a major exhibition of modern Cuban painting was staged at the Museum of Modern Art in New York. . . . [T]he Museum of Modern art actually acquired Cuban works, most notably Lam's *The Jungle* in 1945. These initiatives were part of a larger programme of Latin American exhibitions and acquisitions, in keeping with President Roosevelt's Good Neighbour policy. After the war Cuban art also found its way to Europe. In 1951, for instance, there was a major exhibition of Cuban art at the Musée National d'Art Moderne in Paris.[5]

The promotion of Haitian painters would benefit enormously from this emerging international appreciation of Caribbean art. The Cuban painter Wilfredo Lam is perhaps a key figure in the explosion of interest in Haitian primitivism. Not only did Lam's work reflect Afro-Caribbean iconography with its obvious references to the divinities of the Santeria religion in Cuba, but Lam himself spent some time at the Centre d'Art and exhibited there.

Given the embattled nature of the cultural scene in Haiti in the 1940s and the tensions that divided the society, it is arguably only an American visitor to Haiti like Dewitt Peters who could have got the Centre d'Art started. A project of this nature needed both government support and sponsorship in order to exist. The pro-U.S. president at the time, Elie Lescot, did not hesitate, when approached by Peters, to acquire an old house in Port-au-Prince to house the center and to refurbish the building. The first exhibition of paintings at the center was also the first comprehensive exhibition of painting in Port-au-Prince. Held in 1944, it was officially opened by Lescot and was a great social and financial success. The Haitian government then increased its subsidy to the center, and the U.S. State Department also provided a subsidy. Up this point, the Centre d'Art mostly sponsored work by Haiti's early modernists and did not exhibit any paintings by self-taught artists.

Six months after the center opened, however, a painting by a then unknown artist from northern Haiti, Philomé Obin, was sent to the center. Peters, who by his own admission had taken no interest in "primitive" painting up to this point, bought the painting and communicated with Obin, who turned out to be a serious artist whose ambition was to record Haiti's history in paint. Word of the center's acquisition spread, and soon Peters found himself handing out pieces of cardboard to another self-taught artist, Rigaud Benoît, who eventually painted one of the murals of the St. Trinity cathedral. Perhaps the greatest discovery at this time was the work of Hector Hippolyte, whose work was spotted quite accidentally on the door of a small bar in a little village. When Hippolyte was eventually found, it turned out that he had become a housepainter in a desperate effort to survive. Hippolyte died a few years later, but not before doing a number of mystical paintings for the center and achieving international recognition after the visit of André Breton to Haiti. Similar discoveries of self-taught artists were made, such as Castera Bazile, who worked as Peters' houseboy, and Wilson Bigaud, whose large, impressive painting "Paradis Terrestre" represented the summit of individual achievement at this time.

In 1947 the American travel writer Selden Rodman became co-director of the Centre d'Art. The publication of his book on Haitian primitive art,

Renaissance in Haiti (1948), the first of many works championing Haitian popular artists, further enhanced the reputation of Haitian primitivism abroad, especially in the United States. Patronage for the primitive painters came mostly from outside Haiti—from Europe and, increasingly, North America. This raised controversial issues within Haiti and in the Centre d'Art in particular. There were those in the elite who felt that once more Haitian culture was being stereotyped in terms of a kind of an alluring barbarity. There were others who felt that Haitian modernism, which had predated the success of the self-taught artists, was being marginalized. It was also felt that the label "primitive" put excessive emphasis on the unspoilt nature of the painters and reduced them to a uniformly anonymous mass. Such a label ignored the diversity of styles and artistic awareness that existed among the artists labeled primitive. These tensions exploded in 1950 when a group of artists, made up mostly of the modernists who had helped found the Centre d'Art, broke with the center to start their own gallery called the Foyer des Arts Plastiques (Center for Visual Arts). This alternative center sought to promote a kind of Haitian modernism, in contrast to Peters' and Rodman's emphasis on authenticity and purity. The project had no chance of succeeding in the face of the runaway success of the Centre d'Art project. Soon some the best artists of the breakaway group, such as its founder, Max Pinchinnat, and Roland Dorcely, left Haiti for Paris and the movement began to wither.

The split in the Centre d'Art was perhaps inevitable, given the divergent paths of the two main artistic schools, the modernists and the primitives. Without Peters and later Rodman, the peasant painters would not have been discovered. Hippolyte and Obin were in their late forties when their work appeared in Peter's center. They had no encouragement or recognition during the twenty years that they tried to paint. However, the primitivist label tended to obscure the diverse talents, experiences, and sensibilities that existed among these artists. Many were more artistically self-conscious than others and were aware of Haitian artistic traditions that pre-existed their discovery by the Centre d'Art.

Philomé Obin (1892–1986) is an example of a so-called primitive artist who seemed very aware of Haitian history and was clearly attentive to the tradition of official patriotic art. His work consists of meticulously painted scenes of the Haitian revolution, the fathers of Haitian independence, and scenes of Cap-Haïtien, where he spent his life. Despite the many years of neglect, Obin regarded himself as a professional painter. He had had some art training when he was young and regarded his work as an accurate record of Haitian history or social reality. What made his work interesting is that, despite his feeling that his work was classical, the subtle distortions and departures from classical technique produce a true originality in his paintings. His two best-known works, "The Crucifixion of Charlemagne Peralte" and "The Funeral of Charlemagne Peralte" are both on the same theme, the death of the Caco (guerrilla) leader Charlemagne Peralte during the U.S. occupation. As a whale, his paintings have a dispassionate formality, but in the case of these two there is a sense of emotional involvement in the guerrilla leader's death that is unmistakable. Obin managed a branch of the Centre d'Art in Cap Haitien and became the leader of the patriotic school of northern Haiti.

Quite different from the more mainstream and technically sophisticated Obin is the other great discovery of the Centre d'Art, Hector Hippolyte (1894–1948). His work, which like Obin's long pre-existed Peters' center, fits more closely the label of primitive authenticity that these painters had acquired. His paintings are invariably visionary and vaudou-inspired. With Hippolyte, Obin's revolutionary and patriotic iconography yields to a surreal mysticism. Hippolyte used enamel house paint and a brush made of chicken feathers to achieve a spectacular inventiveness in works that won the enthusiastic endorsement of the surrealists André Breton and Wifredo Lam. The naivete and directness of his style won him many foreign admirers. His most compelling paintings were drawn from the visions he experienced during possession. These pictures are dominated by the depictions of the various *loas*. All other decoration is subordinated to the figure of the deity, who is usually evoked in bold, fiery colors. This is evident in his best-known and most symmetrical work, "The Three-Eyed King," which was, in its depiction of a double-nosed and three-eyed god, Hippolyte's vision of the chief god of Haitian vaudou, le bon Dieu.

Even though it would be a simplification to see all the works of the Haitian primitives as vaudou-derived—Obin was, after all a practicing Protestant—it is true that the iconography of the vaudou religion provided the basis for the visionary power of this painting. Another artist who was also a *houngan* was Robert St. Brice (1898–1973). He also painted the *loas*, but his more spectral figures were evoked with less crude directness than Hippolyte's. Similarly, Rigaud Benoît (1911–1986), Peters' chauffeur, first painted typical Haitian scenes for the tourist trade but produced his most startling pictures from vaudou themes. His work has more variety than that of Hippolyte or St. Brice because he often turned to anecdotal subjects, satirizing aspects of Haitian social life. Another one of the important early primitives was Castera Bazile (1923–1964). Bazile was markedly different from the sometimes irreverent Benoit. His work was consistently religious, with his most memorable themes drawn from biblical scenes, and it is not surprising that he was one of the main artists involved with the decoration of the St. Trinity cathedral. This devotional element in his work gave way at times to scenes of stoic suffering among Haiti's poor.

The most accomplished of the artists at the Centre d'Art was Wilson Bigaud (b. 1931), whose work dominates the murals of St. Trinity. Without the strong religious convictions of the other self-taught painters and more technically advanced, Bigaud painted a number of dramatizations of Haitian folk culture: cockfights, wakes, and vaudou ceremonies. However, when asked to participate in the St. Trinity project, he chose the scene of Christ turning water into wine at the wedding in Cana. He produced a teeming, colorful, Breughel-like depiction of the biblical scene, which is one of the most spectacular of the St. Trinity murals. He is closer to Hippolyte than to Obin in his dramatic use of color. Apart from the wedding at Cana, the other painting for which Bigaud is famous was his "Paradis Terrestre," which was acquired by the Museum of Modern Art in New York in 1950. His canvases always exhibited a bustling realism. They were invariably crowded with figures of daily life in Haiti, all drenched in a glowing light. After a nervous breakdown in 1958, Bigaud was never able to return to his earlier creativity.

In a completely different category are the somber, brooding canvases of Jacques Enguerrand Gourgue (1931). Neither realistic nor religious, Gourgue dealt with themes that were mystical or quite simply drawn from black magic. His iconography was drawn from the Haitian unconscious, an infernal world of werewolves, demons, snakes, *bocors*, and pierced bodies. He stands out among the generally brightly lit canvases of the primitives with the sinister atmosphere his painting evokes and the eerie themes of devil worship and sacrifice. His work "The Magic Table" is also part of the Museum of Modern Art's permanent collection. This tormented sensibility, which sometimes evoked a nightmarish Salvador Dali, received worldwide recognition in the 1960s and 1970s through exhibits in North America and Europe.

Far more benign and symmetrical is the style of Prefete Duffaut (b. 1923) who is best known for his paintings of fantastic cities. Duffaut's work is known for its unusual organization of space and the visionary presentation of cities floating in a blue void. An early member of the Centre d'Art, he is not known for the depiction of religious themes. The one exception to this characteristic is his 1959 painting "Heaven and Hell," which depicts these two opposed worlds sprouting like trees from the earth. In general, his paintings are graphic and colorful representations of the extremely mountainous terrain around Jacmel, with its sharp mountain peaks and tortuously winding roads. His paintings look like surreal maps that depict all subjects frontally and in excruciating detail. From the zigzagging streets and conelike mountain peaks to crowded streets, there is no attempt made to suggest depth or perspective.

Even though it is clearly erroneous to see Haitian art labeled "primitive" as vaudou-inspired, vaudou has produced much of the arresting iconography of Haitian art. Because of the importance of visual representation in that religion, from ground painting to the images of Catholic saints, *houngans* in particular were generally adept at some form of visual representation. Consequently, in the tradition of Hector Hippolyte, a later phase of vaudou-derived art emerged in which André Pierre (b. 1916) was the most outstanding figure. Pierre, a practicing vaudou priest from Croix-des-Missions, was encouraged to paint by the American filmmaker and self-styled ethnologist Maya Deren. It took him some time to apply what he saw as a divine gift to the secular art of painting. In 1959 he decided to move from his decorations of temple walls, sacred bottles, and calabashes to devote himself entirely to painting. His work could well have been influenced by earlier self-taught painters from the Centre d'Art like Hippolyte and Bigaud, who had completed their major work by this time. Pierre painted at a time when the only unthreatened figures in Haiti were the *hougans* and the primitive artists, of which he was both. His paintings all predictably deal with vaudou deities; Agoue was Pierre's favorite *loa*. His paintings are marked by a spectacular display of shooting stars and blazing comets. Despite the high level of Pierre's achievement, it was clear that as the years went by Haitian primitive art was becoming the victim of its own success. Pierre's work became repetitive and predictable as the commissions and increasingly high fees poured in. After the wave of *dechoukaj* of 1986, when vaudou associated with Duvalierism was attacked, Pierre's elaborately decorated temple was flattened.

No account of the primitivism in Haitian art or of the aesthetic legacy of vaudou can be complete without reference to the metalworkers of Haitian popular art. In contrast to the vast majority of wood carvings from Haiti, which were invariably grotesque "African" masks destined for the gullible tourist trade, the *feronniers*, or blacksmiths, brought a new creativity to Haitian sculpture. The first of these to achieve recognition was Georges Liautaud (1899–1992), a blacksmith at Croix-de-Bouquets. Liautaud had trained as a railway mechanic in the Dominican Republic, and in Haiti he started making metal crosses for graves. The first examples of his work that were noticed were his iron crosses, which looked like *veves*. The cross, which became the basic form for much of his early work, depicted the intricate relationship that existed in vaudou mythology between life and death.

In 1953 his work was brought to the attention of the Centre d'Art, which encouraged Liautaud to pursue his more visionary ideas. In his later sculptures he turned toward depicting figures from vaudou mythology. Before him no metal sculpture existed in Haiti, and he pioneered the technique of using flattened metal drums as his material for sculpting. The shapes were drawn on the metal surface, then cut out with a hammer and chisel, and finally coated with a film of varnish. For larger figures, an entire side of a metal drum was beaten flat and then shaped with metal shears or a hacksaw. Some of Liautaud's favorite subjects were the *sirene*, or mermaid, Erzulie, and the sacred twins, or *marasa*. His fantasy sculptures are often made up of forms that constantly seem to change from fish to human to animal. In so doing he captured in metal the fluid metamorphosis that existed in the realm of the spiritual for the vaudou worshiper.

A group of sculptors gathered around Liautaud at Croix des Bouquets. The use of shears on recycled oil drums and welded sections became the order of the day among the younger metalworkers. Three of these younger artists have become famous in their own right. Gabriel Bien Aimé (b. 1951) was a car mechanic who turned to metal sculpture. His work has acquired a three-dimensional effect by twisting parts of the metal. His contemporary, Serge Jolimeau, also born in 1951, uses vaudou motifs in his work; it often exhibits an eroticism absent from his master's designs, often ingeniously creating a layered, mobile effect through the use of hooks and chains. Another major disciple of Liautaud is Murat Brierre (b. 1938). His work had more range and sophistication from the outset, and as a rule he tends to treat biblical subjects. The Garden of Eden is a favorite subject, and one of his best works is the crucifixion series. The fact that he started off as a painter is evident in the complex figures and the narrative element frequently represented in his sculpture.

MODERN TRENDS

After 1957, artistic creation in Haiti faced two dilemmas, one internal and the other external. All artists had to confront the repressiveness of Duvalier's dictatorial regime within Haiti. On the outside, the degrading effect of an indiscriminate North American market on self-taught artists had resulted an uncreative repetitiveness. The lack of freedom of expression under the Duvaliers produced a kind of technically sophisticated but essentially escapist formalism among painters in the 1960s and 1970s. Painters who belonged to a group of artists associated with the School of Beauty produced a number of pleasing works that incorporated modernist styles with local themes. This highly decorative art had none of the element of social protest that had stimulated early artists like Pétion Savain's group. These paintings found a local market among the Duvalierist elite and were particularly favored by the entourage of Jean Claude and Michele Duvalier. Their paintings had, after all, won much respect among foreign collectors, carried no political message, and did not reveal the any of the disturbing aspects of Haiti's social reality.

Four major artists of this group were Bernard Séjourné (1947–1994), Lyonel Laurenceau (b. 1942), Emilcar Simil (b. 1944), and Jean-René Jérôme (1942–1991). Séjourné was a member of Haiti's business elite who had an apparently inexhaustible capacity to integrate diverse modern techniques into his work. He spent most of his time turning the humble peasantry into majestic icons and generally embellishing the Haitian countryside with a marketable magical realism for the cocktail circuit crowd. In a similar vein, Simil single-mindedly insisted on an aesthetic formalism in his paintings. He is known for his paintings of jet-black figures decorated with gold jewelry and patterned silk. He sees himself as Haiti's answer to the Viennese painter Gustav Klimt. Laurenceau, on the other hand, shows much greater empathy for the poor of Haiti than do his contemporaries. He has a gift for symbolically manipulating quite realistic scenes and figures drawn from Haitian social reality. However, he invariably sanitizes his images with an overpowering sentimentality that makes him fit perfectly into the formalism of the School of Beauty. Jerome's work is the most personal of the four painters in this group. His effects are always elegant, with a fluid transparency achieved in his canvases.

All four painters did well commercially and were the only group of mainstream painters to challenge the success of the self-taught artists. However, their success came at a cost, as commercialization increased the ornamental quality of work, which invariably was lacking in depth. The only prominent artist of this generation who is an exception to this trend towards empty aestheticism is Bernard Wah (1939–1981). There is a violent and disturbing element in Wah's work that sets him apart from the School of Beauty and arguably makes him an heir of the socially engaged experimentation of the Foyer des Arts Plastiques. A graphic and lurid dimension in the abstract forms he conjured up seemed to indirectly reflect the painful experience of the Duvalier years. He made a short-lived attempt to establish his own artistic movement, which he called "Calfou." He eventually left Haiti and settled in New York in 1966.

The only group that managed to pursue a genuinely experimental agenda during the Duvalier years was the Poto-Mitan group. The group drew its name from the main support in the vaudou temple, literally "the pole in the middle." The group was founded by Jean-Claude Garoute, also known as

Tiga (b. 1935); Patrick Vilaire (b. 1942); and Wilfrid Austin, also known as Frido (b. 1945). Their work was admittedly apolitical, but they tried to devise new artistic forms based on pre-Columbian artifacts and vaudou iconography. Their sometimes mystical theories pushed them to experimentation in painting as well as ceramics and sculpture. Patrick Vilaire was the most accomplished sculptor in the group. Their work as a whole was not as commercially successful as that of the painters of the School of Beauty, but it did not sacrifice depth and originality for a facile ornamentation.

Tiga became known in the early 1970s for the work he did with Maud Robart among the St. Soleil group of self-taught painters. This movement stemmed from Tiga's ideas on art and mysticism and was located in a commune in the mountains above Port-au-Prince. Tiga gave materials and paint to members of a community that had never before painted. Out of this experiment came a drama troupe and the rebirth of Haitian popular art, at a time when primitivism had become an exhausted tradition. Prospère Pierre-Louis (1947–1996), the major talent in this group; Levoy Exil (b. 1944); Dieuseul Paul (b. 1953); and Louisianne St. Fleurant (1922), the only Haitian female artist in this tradition, were nonrepresentational in their vaudou-inspired paintings, suggesting the amorphous spirits of St. Brice. Their refusal to make even the slightest concession to realism set them apart from the earlier phase of Haitian primitivism. They developed a distinctive style based on the intricate patterns, outlined in black, that dominate the strange forms in their work.

St. Soleil came to international prominence in 1975 when the French writer and cultural critic André Malraux visited Tiga's commune. He wrote glowingly about the spirituality and the religious iconography of this group of unspoilt painters in his study of religious art *L'intemporel* (The timeless, 1976). In this regard, Malraux was repeating the visit and patronage of Haitian primitive artists by the surrealists in the mid-1940s. Again a Western intellectual's endorsement of the magic of Haitian art brought commercial success to local artists. It also brought about the breakup of the St. Soleil community because painters saw that they could easily make their living outside the commune Tiga had established. The group broke with Tiga by the end of the 1970s, and all went on to sell their work to collectors in Europe and the United States for high prices. St. Soleil revitalized artistic creativity in Haiti and inspired other self-taught artists, such as Stevenson Magloire and Lionel Cineus, once more confirming the view that the Haitian peasantry had a natural talent for painting. Much of this talent today is explicitly politicized, as can be seen in the graffiti that cover walls all over Haiti's capital.

One of the most interesting recent additions to the list of Haitian artists is the novelist Franck Etienne. It is not unusual for Haitian artists to be multitalented. Many are musicians, sculptors, and painters at the same time. However, it is unprecedented for a major novelist to also be a respected painter, but since the 1970s Franck Etienne has been painting with great success. His vibrant and colorful abstract canvases are unmistakable. He is clearly drawn to the Jackson Pollock style of "action painting," with an expressionistic splash of paint and trailing lines of color often suggesting some inner anxiety.

Outside of Haiti, art thrives in the work of Edouard Duval-Carrié, who must be the most impressive professional Haitian artist today. He father is a member of the business class that fled Duvalierism. Duval-Carrié grew up in Puerto Rico and was trained in Canada. After many years in Paris he moved to Miami in order to be closer to Haiti. Duval-Carrié often uses vaudou iconography and evokes the surreal world of vaudou spirituality. He is also known for irreverent canvases that comment satirically on Haitian politics. He has been particularly barbed in his paintings of the Duvalier family; his depiction of Jean-Claude Duvalier in a bridal dress makes humorous references to rumors of the former dictator's sexual preferences. His work represents a surreal chronicle of Haitian history as well as the tragicomedy of the post-Duvalier years. His wicked sense of humor and social awareness connects him to those mainstream artistic traditions in Haiti that attempted to adapt modern techniques to the country's surreal political and social reality.

Some artists born in Haiti have made a name for themselves abroad. However, their work has no explicit connection with the land of their birth. For instance, Hervé Télémaque (b. 1937) may have been born in Haiti, but he has lived for so long in France that he is considered a French artist. His desire for a neutral artistic identity is different from those Haitian artists who have taken a prominent place in North America and remained identifiably Haitian, such as Edwidge Danticat and Wyclef Jean. There is one artist of Haitian origin who made an impact on the U.S. art scene and now is an influence among many young Caribbean artists. Son of a Haitian father, Jean Michel Basquiat (1960–1988) was inspired by the graffiti and street culture created by Caribbean people in New York. His meteoric rise to fame and death from a drug overdose have only strengthened the myth of the self-destructive genius that Basquiat represents. Basquiat also functions like a latter-day Wifredo Lam in his ability to inspire a broad range of Caribbean artists.

Whatever the fate of vaudou as a religious institution, its artistic legacy is enormous in Haiti and has now been fully recognized as an art from outside

Haiti. The murals of the vaudou temple, the bottles on the altars, the sequined vaudou flags, and the luminous chalk white emblems of the gods on the ground of the peristyle are now recognized as part of the popular arts of Haiti. The successful exhibition that toured major cities in the United States, "The Sacred Arts of Haitian Vaudou," was not only an antidote to the demonic image of Haitian religion, but the assembled objects demonstrated the extent to which Haitian artists were masters of color and imaginative inventiveness. The boldness of the popular imagination was as present in the meticulously made flags of Antoine Oleyant as in the fantastic assemblages of recycled market materials embellished with lace and sequins from Pierrot Barra. The success of this exhibition was a clear sign of Haiti's artistic coming of age.

ARCHITECTURE

Even though Haitian writers have waxed lyrical about the charms of the Haitian landscape and the picturesqueness of its people, a visitor to Haiti today will be disappointed to see the poverty and the backwardness of a history of neglect and exploitation. There are few marks made on the Haitian landscape, few buildings constructed, that merit serious comment. Port-au-Prince has never been a great aesthetic experience. A teeming population today overruns it, and there are few signs of the availability of basic human services. Outside Port-au-Prince, towns are monotonous and dust-blown, or simply reduced to a collection of squalid buildings. Haiti's capital is as marked by its spectacular slums as it is by the few monumental structures that survive. The spectacular slums of La Saline or Cité Soleil leave more of an abiding impression than the gleaming white presidential palace that has a marked resemblance to the White House in Washington. Government buildings, such as ministries or the parliament or *palais legislatif*, are functional at best or decrepit at worst. The Roman Catholic cathedral is not a blemish on the rest of the city but has little to recommend it aesthetically. Most commentators agree that there is but one example of breathtaking manmade edifice in Haiti: the Citadelle, built by Henri Christophe, in the north.

Built 3,000 feet above the village of Milot, on a peak so steep that it is known as Le Bonnet de L'Eveque, or the bishop's miter, stands a stone fortress built in the shape of a ship. This towering structure has a commanding view of the northern coastline. On a clear day, you can see Cap-Haïtien and as far as the border with the Dominican Republic. Construction of this fortress may even have started before Henri Christophe became king. However, it was Christophe who in 1807 established control over the north of Haiti, which was ruled as a monarchy. His state prospered under rigorous control. Christophe, who was a practical man in military and economic matters, had a taste for grandeur and magnificence. The Citadelle was not meant to be just an impregnable fortress. It was like the king's castle, Sans Souci, meant to impress the Western world with the new nation's ability to create an astonishing structure. It is difficult to imagine how thousands of workers could have hoisted hundreds of cannons and tons of building material up steep and rocky paths. The structure has an irregular shape with a rounded bastion and a triangular spur at the front that creates the impression of a ship's prow.

The interior is made up of a maze of secret passages, galleries, dungeons, and separate rooms for the cannon. Christophe has envisaged a fortress that could house more than 1,000 men and could withstand a siege of three years. The battlements are three meters thick and the ceilings of the rooms forty meters high. The cannons are still in place today, with massive piles of cannon balls that were never used; these were either made in the king's foundry or captured from the French. There are signs everywhere of the meticulous construction of this architectural marvel. While the construction was in progress, a number of brick and tile factories operated around the clock in order provide the building materials for the workers. Legends abound when it comes to Christophe's Citadelle. It is said that he once ordered a regiment of soldiers to march off over the battlements into the dizzying void below. Another is that after the king's suicide, he was buried upright in one of the walls of the fortification.

Christophe did not only construct this fortress. Down below in that village of Milot, the ruins of the palace Sans Souci can be found. These ruins are evidence of the king's taste for luxurious excess. The exterior of the building is still standing, but an earthquake has destroyed the rest. Christophe established his court in this palace, and the imposing staircases that lead to the entrance of the building with the fountain in the center were meant to suggest the castle of Versailles in France. The other side of the palace has a terrace from which the king apparently reviewed his troops. These displays were meant to further impress Christophe's subjects and the king's visitors with the splendor of Haiti's achievements after independence. In the foreground of Sans Souci, there still can be found a circular, dome-covered chapel where the king regularly attended religious services.

The palace was surrounded by gardens, and its rooms were tastefully furnished with paintings, tapestries, mirrors, and candelabra, for which Christophe had developed a taste while he worked at the Auberge de la Couronne, one of the most fashionable hotels in Cap-Haïtien before independence. The king held audience daily in this palace in his throne room. He would greet foreign dignitaries as well as delegations from all over his kingdom. All activities followed strict rules of etiquette. He was surrounded on these occasions by his courtiers, who had been given the titles of duke, count, and commander. The king has been seen, at various times, as insane or suffering from delusions of grandeur. Many of these explanations for his obsession with fine palaces leave out his construction of barracks and a hospital. The streets of his capital city, Cap-Henri, were also paved, and roads were built that make it equal to any small city in Europe at the time. It is in Sans Souci that the king ended his life deserted by his court and surrounded by his mirrors and chandeliers.

There is little else in the North of Haiti to complete with the grandeur of Christophe's architectural ruins. Cap-Haïtien's silver domed cathedral is no match for the king's grandiose imagination. The relative decline of the city after the Haitian state established Port-au-Prince as the nation's capital as well as natural disasters has left little of the early wooden buildings of the nineteenth century that add to the ragged charm of such provincial cities as Jacmel in the south. Consequently, the city that was burnt by Christophe during the war of independence, rebuilt as Cap-Henri and then destroyed by earthquakes and hurricanes is a far cry from its dazzling past, when it was referred to as "little Paris." A final indignity was visited on the city during the U.S. occupation when the Marines changed the original French street names and substituted letters for streets parallel to the ocean and numbers for streets running in the opposite direction. Nevertheless, the fact that northern Haiti has monopolized the major events of Haitian history seems to have left a mark of graciousness on the northern city that Port-au-Prince does not have. It was here in the north that Toussaint L'Ouverture was born, that Boukman led the first rebellion and that the Bois Caiman is located. A recent visitor, looking across the north from the ramparts of the Citadelle, describes as "one of the most magnificent scenes in all the world"[6] the panoramic mix of majestic mountain and grand ruins.

NOTES

1. Harold Courlander, *The Drum and the Hoe: Life and Lore of the Haitian People* (Berkeley: University of California Press, 1960).

2. Selden Rodman, *Haiti: The Black Republic* (New York: Devin Air, 1954).

3. Jean Price-Mars, *So Spoke the Uncle*, trans. Magdaline Shannon (Washington, D.C.: Three Continents Press, 1983), 182.

4. Alfred Metraux, *Voodoo in Haiti* (London: Andre Deutsch, 1959), 343.

5. Veerle Poupeye *Caribbean Art* (London: Thames and Hudson, 1998), 64.

6. Ian Thompson, *Bonjour Blanc: A Journey Through Haiti* (London: Penguin, 1993), 381.

Bibliography

Abbott, Elizabeth. *Haiti: The Duvaliers and Their Legacy*. New York: McGraw Hill, 1988.

Alexis, Jacques Stephen. *General Sun, My Brother*. Trans. Carrol F. Coates. Charlottesville: University Press of Virginia, 1999.

Arthur, Charles, and Michael Dash. *Libete: A Haitian Anthology*. New York: Markus Weiner, 1999.

Averill, Gage. *A Day for the Hunter, A Day for the Prey: Popular Music and Power in Haiti*. Chicago: University of Chicago Press, 1997.

Banks, Russell. *Continental Drift*. New York: Harper and Row, 1985.

Bastien, Remy. "Vodoun and Politics in Haiti." In *Religion and Politics in Haiti*. Washington, DC: Institute for Cross-Cultural Research, 1966.

Bellegarde-Smith, Patrick. *Haiti: The Breached Citadel*. Boulder, CO: Westview Press, 1990.

Bloncourt, Gerald, and Marie Jose Nadal-Gardere. *La Peinture Haïtienne/Haitian Arts*. Paris: Ediciones Nathan, 1986.

Bohning, Don. "Haiti Risking Loss of Support As Crisis Festers." *Miami Herald*, October 8, 1998.

Brown, Karen McCarthy. *Mama Lola: A Vodou Priestess in Brooklyn*. Berkeley: University of California Press, 1991.

Buch, Hans Christoph. *The Wedding in Port-au-Prince*. London: Faber and Faber, 1987.

Carpentier, Alejo. *The Kingdom of This World*. London: Penguin, 1980.

Cave, Hugh B. *Haiti: High Road to Adventure*. New York: Holt, 1952.

Cham, Mbaye. *Ex-Iles: Essays on Caribbean Cinema*. Trenton, NJ: Africa World Press, 1992.

Chambers, Frances. *Haiti*. World Bibliographic Series, Santa Barbara, CA: Clio Press, 1983.

Clitandre, Pierre. *Cathedral of the August Heat*. Trans. Bridget Jones. London: Readers International, 1987.

Consentino, Donald J. *Sacred Arts of Haitian Vodou*. Los Angeles: UCLA Fowler Museum of Cultural History, 1995.

Corvington, Georges. *Port-au-Prince au cours des ans: La ville contemporaine*. Port-au-Prince: Henri Deschamps, 1991.

Courlander, Harold. *The Drum and the Hoe: Life and Lore of the Haitian People*. Berkeley: University of California Press, 1960.

Craige, John Houston. *Cannibal Cousins*. New York: Minton, Balch, 1934.

Danner, Mark. "Beyond the Mountains." *New Yorker*, November 27, 1989, 55–100.

Danticat, Edwidge. *Breath, Eyes, Memory*. New York: Soho Press, 1994.

———. *The Farming of Bones*. New York: Soho Press, 1998.

Dash, J. Michael. *Literature and Ideology in Haiti (1915–1961)*. Totowa, NJ: Barnes and Noble, 1981.

———. *Haiti and the United States: National Stereotypes and the Literary Imagination*. New York: St. Martin's Press, 1997.

———. *The Other America: Caribbean Literature in a New World Context*. Charlottesville: University Press of Virginia, 1998.

Davis, Wade. *The Serpent and the Rainbow*. London: Collins, 1986.

Dayan, Joan. *Haiti, History and the Gods*. Berkeley: University of California Press, 1995.

Depestre, Rene. "La revolution de 1946 est pour demain," In *1946–1976 Trente ans de pouvoir Noir en Haiti*. Lasalle: Collectif Paroles, 1976.

———. *The Festival of the Greasy Pole*. Trans. Carrol F. Coates. Charlottesville: University Press of Virginia, 1990.

Deren, Maya. *The Voodoo Gods*. London: Thames and Hudson, 1953.

Desmangles, Leslie. *The Faces of the Gods: Vaudou and Roman Catholicism in Haiti*. Chapel Hill: University of North Carolina Press, 1992.

Diederich, Bernard, and Al Burt. *Papa Doc: The Truth about Haiti Today*. New York: McGraw-Hill, 1969.

Dunham, Katherine. *Island Possessed*. Garden City, NY: Doubleday, 1969.

Dupuy, Alex. *Haiti in the World Economy: Class, Race and Underdevelopment Since 1700*. Boulder, CO: Westview Press, 1989.

Farmer, Paul. *The Uses of Haiti*. Munroe, ME: Common Courage Press, 1994.

Ferguson, James. *Papa Doc, Baby Doc*. Oxford, England: Blackwell, 1987.

Fleischmann, Ulrich. "The Formation of a Literary Discourse: One, Two or Three Literatures." In *A History of Literature in the Caribbean*, ed. A. James Arnold. Amsterdam: John Benjamins, 1994.

Gold, Herbert. *Best Nightmare on Earth: A Life in Haiti*. London: Grafton Books, 1991.

Greene, Graham. *The Comedians*. Harmondsworth: Penguin, 1967.

Heinl, Robert Debs. *Written in Blood: The Story of the Haitian People*. New York: Houghton Mifflin, 1978.

Herskovitz, Melville. *Life in a Haitian Valley*. New York: Knopf, 1937.

Hoffmann, Léon François. *Essays on Haitian Literature*. Washington, DC: Three Continents Press, 1984.

Hunt, Alfred. *Haiti's Influence on Antebellum America*. Baton Rouge: Louisiana State University Press, 1998.

Hurarska, Anna. "The First Casualty," *New Yorker*, April 19, 1993.

Hurston, Zora Neale. *Tell My Horse*. Philadelphia: Lippincott, 1938.

James, C.L.R. *The Black Jacobins: Toussaint Louverture and the San Domingo Revolution*. New York: Vintage Books, 1963.

Laferrière, Dany. *An Aroma of Coffee*. Trans. David Homel. Toronto: Coach House Press, 1993.

Laguerre, Michel. *American Odyssey: Haitians in New York City*. Ithaca, NY: Cornell University Press, 1984.

———. *Diasporic Citizenship: Haitian Americans in Transnational America*. New York: St. Martin's, 1998.

Lawless, Robert. *Haiti's Bad Press*. Rochester, VT: Shenckman, 1992.

Leyburn, James. *The Haitian People*. Rev. ed. New Haven, CT: Yale University Press, 1966.

Metellus, Jean. *The Vortex Family*. Trans. Michael Richardson. London: Peter Owen, 1995.

McLane, Daisann. "The Haitian Beat Thrives in Times of Suffering." *The New York Times*, March 8, 1992.

Metraux, Alfred. *Voodoo in Haiti*. London: Andre Deutsch, 1959.

Montague, Ludwell Lee. *Haiti and the United States 1714–1938*. Durham, NC: Duke University Press, 1940.

Moore, Brian. *No Other Life*. New York: Doubleday, 1993.

Moreau de St. Mery, Louis Elie. *A Civilization That Perished: The Last Years of White Colonial Rule in Haiti*. Trans. Ivor Spenser. Lanham, MD: University Press of America, 1985.

Nicholls, David. *From Dessalines to Duvalier: Race, Colour and Independence in Haiti*. Cambridge: Cambridge University Press, 1979.

———. *Haiti in Caribbean Context: Ethnicity, Economy, and Revolt*. London: Macmillan, 1985.

Pierre, Gary Pierre. "For Haitians, Leadership Split Is a Generation Gap," *New York Times*, September 24, 1997. Online.

Plummer, Brenda. *Haiti and the Great Powers 1902–1915*. Baton Rouge: Louisiana State University Press, 1988.

Poupeye, Veerle. *Caribbean Art*. London: Thames and Hudson, 1998.

Price-Mars, Jean. *So Spoke the Uncle*. Trans. Magdaline Shannon. Washington, DC: Three Continents Press, 1983.

Rodman, Selden. *Haiti: The Black Republic*. New York: Devin Adair, 1954.

————. *Where Art Is Joy: Haitian Art the First Forty Years*. New York: Ruggles de la Tour, 1988.

Rohter, Larry. "Rooting Up Fears: Haitian Farmers Fill the Silos," *New York Times*, February 3, 1995. Online.

Roumain, Jacques. *Masters of the Dew*. Trans. Langston Hughes and Mercer Cook. London: Heinemann, 1978.

Sartre, Jean-Paul. "Orphée noir." In *Anthologie de la nouvelle poésie nègre et malgache de langue française*, ed. L. S. Senghor. Paris: Presses Universitaires de France, 1948.

Schmidt, Hans. *The United States Occupation of Haiti*. New Brunswick, NJ: Rutgers University Press, 1971.

Seabrook, William. *The Magic Island*. New York: Harcourt Brace, 1929.

Thompson, Ian. *Bonjour Blanc: A Journey Through Haiti*. London: Penguin, 1993.

Thompson, Robert Farris. *Flask of the Spirit*. New York: Random House, 1984.

Trouillot, Michel Rolph. *Haiti, State Against Nation: The Origins and Legacy of Duvalierism*. New York: Monthly Review Press, 1990.

Weinstein, Brian, and Aaron Segal. *Haiti: Political Failures, Cultural Successes*. New York: Praeger, 1984.

Wilentz, Amy. *The Rainy Season: Haiti Since Duvalier*. New York: Touchstone, 1989.

Wucker, Michele. *Why the Cocks Fight: Dominicans, Haitians, and the Struggle for Hispaniola*. New York: Hill and Wang, 1999.

Index

About the Author

J. MICHAEL DASH is a Professor of French at New York University, and is a specialist of Haitian culture and literature.